'This book is a powerful testar[...] who has suffered greatly.'

Alexander McCall Smith

'*Unbroken* stands testament to the fact that it's not what happens to you in this life that counts, but how you respond to those happenings. Madeleine is an example to us all that we need not be defined by actions inflicted upon us by others, but we can instead be shaped and indeed strengthened by our experiences, good or bad.'

Lorraine McIntosh, Deacon Blue

'It is not easy to read Madeleine Black's story, but it is vital that you do. It is a book to buy and pass on, a book to borrow, a book to recommend. *Unbroken* is a story to help deepen our understanding of what we are capable of: depravity and compassion, horror and survival, and ultimately, a better future.'

Gary Lewis, actor

'It is deeply moving to stay with the twists and turns of this brave, educative narrative as the author gradually confronts her frozen pain and speaks out about what it has taken for her to grow into her strength as a vibrant woman, trusting her place in the world. This book is a generous, hard-won gift that will inspire and heal many others.'

Marian Partington, author of *If You Sit Very Still* and fellow speaker for The Forgiveness Project

'Privileged and humbled, these are the words that entered my mind as I read, no, as I lived the journey of Madeleine Black. This is a journey of hope. Thank you, thank you, thank you.'

Peter Woolf, author of *The Damage Done*

'It's not easy to write about pain, let alone rape, but in her remarkable and heartfelt memoir Madeleine Black manages to transform a brutal and traumatic true story into one of meaning and hope.'

Marina Cantacuzino, founder of The Forgiveness Project

'Madeleine Black's Unbroken reveals the horrific trauma of rape and all of its repercussions with fearless honesty, while guiding the reader through such challenging material with an indomitable hope. This beautifully written work is a must-read for men and women alike, and graced with the power to diminish the illusion of our separation that rape and all other violence stems from.'

Arno Arr Michaelis IV, author, director of
Serve 2 Unite, former white supremacist

Unbroken

Unbroken

Used, beaten but *never* broken.
My story of survival and hope.

MADELEINE BLACK

JOHN BLAKE

Published by John Blake Publishing Ltd
3 Bramber Court, 2 Bramber Road,
London W14 9PB, England

www.johnblakebooks.com

www.facebook.com/johnblakebooks ▪
twitter.com/jblakebooks ▪

First published in paperback in 2017

ISBN: 978 1 78606 276 5

British Library Cataloguing-in-Publication Data:

A catalogue record for this book is available from the British Library.

Design by www.envydesign.co.uk

Printed in Great Britain by CPI Group (UK) Ltd

1 3 5 7 9 10 8 6 4 2

Papers used by John Blake Publishing are natural, recyclable products made from
wood grown in sustainable forests. The manufacturing processes conform to the
environmental regulations of the country of origin.

Every attempt has been made to contact the relevant copyright-holders,
but some were unobtainable. We would be grateful if the appropriate
people could contact us.

John Blake Publishing is an imprint of Bonnier Publishing
www.bonnierpublishing.com

For those who cannot find their voice yet

CONTENTS

'I can be changed by what happens to me.
But I refuse to be reduced by it.'
MAYA ANGELOU

CHAPTER ONE

ONE NIGHT

It happened in May 1979, in North London, where I grew up. The exact date is something I have never tried to establish. Some of what happened to me was very clear in my mind, but most details were hazy, disjointed or gone altogether. It took many years and a lot of hard work to unravel and examine all the details from that night. For decades, I shut the memories out, burying them in my mind beneath a mountain of guilt, fear and self-preservation. And yet even though I didn't consciously think about or remember most of the violence done to me, all of my consequent actions were shaped and influenced by it. I was thirteen years old.

Like many girls I knew, my priorities in life were pretty straightforward: friends, fun, school and boys. My parents were loving and supportive and most of the time I got on well with my older brother and three younger sisters. I tried to help out at home as much as possible and I kept quiet. A shy girl, I was never one to bring a lot of attention to myself. My grades were average and by all means, I was pretty 'normal'. But my friend Kelly was something different altogether.

Almost everyone has that one person in their class that they look up to and want to be like. For me, it was Kelly. She seemed so different from the rest of us and in many ways, she was. Her parents were divorced and I had never met anyone from a single-parent family before. Her dad was American, which seemed exotic at the time, and she wore make-up. She had Farrah Fawcett flicks in her hair and wore far cooler clothes than anyone else in school. Outgoing and flirtatious with boys, she was far more mature and physically developed than most girls in my class. She seemed so bold, so fearless. I was on the other end of the spectrum from Kelly, but being friends with her made me cool.

My dad was always unsure of Kelly and didn't like our friendship for all the same reasons that I found her so intriguing. He felt she was a bad influence on me; I just thought she was fun. The fact that Dad didn't approve of our friendship appealed to the rebel in me – I was, after all, a teenager.

Even though our family got along well, the dynamic in our home at that time was quite difficult. My mum was ill with neck and back problems following a car accident many years ago, and had to spend a lot of time in hospital having operations and recuperating. When she came home, she was often in bed for weeks, even months. There was a rotation of nurses in the house looking after Mum, and between my siblings, my father and me, we did what needed to be done around the house, but it was very stressful.

Perhaps all of those factors contributed to my desire for some fun and excitement. And this in turn led me to do things I might not have done otherwise. To be honest, I think I would have agreed to most things Kelly might have suggested – I was so influenced by her and so ready for something to shake up my day-to-day life. So when she asked if I wanted to go out to drink and meet boys, my response was immediate: Yes, please. I had never done that before, but I was ready. Or so I thought.

Kelly and I started planning our night out. In order to make sure we could stay out as late as we wanted, we pulled off what we thought was a very clever scheme. Kelly was staying with her grandma while her mother was out of town. She told her grandma she would be staying over at my house and I told my mum we would be staying over at Kelly's grandma's. Of course this was before the day when parents would call each other to check the stories, or verify their child's location through the GPS in their mobile phone, so it all worked perfectly. We met up at her mother's vacant flat, dropped off our things and set out to buy some alcohol. My parents weren't big drinkers so I had no idea what to buy; my friend suggested vodka, which she paid for, so I agreed.

Kelly said she knew of an off-licence near a Mexican café on the Finchley Road in North London, just walking distance from where we were staying. We would buy the alcohol there, and then head a few doors down to the café where a lot of boys from the local American school in St John's Wood hung out. Not only did she know some of them from previous times at the café, they were all friends with the manager, who was also American. She assured me it was a safe place for us to drink and meet boys. Perfect.

The first part of the plan went without a hitch. I have no idea how Kelly convinced the shop assistant that she was eighteen (I clearly looked underage), but she did, and so we emerged proudly from the shop with a bottle of vodka and two cartons of orange juice. We excitedly walked to the restaurant, ordered our food, and I followed her to a table where four American boys were sitting. She seemed to know them, but I didn't know how well, so it looked like the second part of our plan (meeting boys) was working perfectly, too.

But then there was a shift I hadn't expected. Within moments, I noticed that Kelly had transformed into a side of her personality I hadn't seen before. She had suddenly developed an American accent and was flirting with the boys in a way that made me feel alienated and embarrassed. It was as though she was performing. Even though she was outgoing, this part of her was a new level of bold, and I became seemingly invisible to her. Naturally, it had an effect on me. I was already too shy to even speak to them, let alone flirt with them, and we were the only girls at the table. It was fun, but I was uneasy and Kelly's behaviour only amplified my discomfort.

Under the cover of the table, we mixed the vodka into our orange juice cartons and then, as much as possible, carried on as if they were normal, un-spiked drinks. Of course, customers weren't allowed to bring in alcohol, let alone underage customers, but breaking the rules was part of the fun. The boys were completely on board – they liked that we brought the vodka. They would let us know when the staff weren't looking and encouraged us to drink it when the coast was clear. At the time, we thought no one on the staff knew we were drinking alcohol. Later, it turned out that at least one of them did know, but chose to look the other way so we could have our fun. However, the boys didn't drink any alcohol – they seemed quite happy to just encourage us.

For a time, everything was going well. There was a lot of laughter and I was beginning to relax a bit (the vodka was helping). But I was slim and had never drunk before, so it didn't take long for the alcohol to affect me. I was nervous and had been drinking quickly as a result. Before I had even finished my carton of spiked orange juice, the room began to spin around and I became tearful. I told Kelly that I was going to be sick and I wanted to go home, but she was having too much fun and wanted to stay. Besides, she probably didn't know I felt as bad as I did. Before I could stand up and go to the toilet, I vomited all over the table.

In an instant, everything changed. The boys were laughing loudly at me and teasing me. None of them made a motion to help me. I may have been nervous and felt some pressure, but now I was an object of ridicule. It was no longer any fun at all. All the noise they made drew over the manager, Mark. He told Kelly and the boys that they needed to get me out of the café quickly because he would get into trouble if he were caught with anyone drinking in there. I felt humiliated, but worse than that, I felt a lack of control I'd never experienced before – I was quickly losing total function of my body.

When I tried to stand up, my legs wouldn't work. I threw up again, this time all over myself. I was vaguely aware of there being customers at other tables in the café, but was really too drunk to notice their reactions. Mark and two of the boys from our table mostly carried me out of the front door of the café and around the side of the building to an alleyway, lined with rubbish bins. Kelly followed us. I could hardly hold myself upright as I slumped against the wall while they decided what to do with me. Mark said that I had to sober up a bit before going home. He, Kelly and the two boys remained there. I don't know what happened to the other two boys who were with us – I never saw them again.

Compared to the boys at our table, who were roughly seventeen years old, Mark was a bit older, maybe in his mid-twenties. He had been flirting with me all night in the café, and it seemed the more uncomfortable I became, the more he carried on. And now, from the outside, it may have appeared that he was just helping me, but while I was leaning unsteadily up against the wall, I was aware, despite how drunk I was, that he was taking advantage of the state I was in. His hands were wandering all over me while he was cleaning me up, and even while getting me to drink some water, but I was just focused on staying on my feet.

Meanwhile, Kelly was still talking and laughing with the other boys; her attention was not on me at all. Clearly she wasn't as drunk as me – she was still able to walk, talk and flirt, it seemed. And it didn't take long before Mark got more aggressive towards me. He kissed me and forced his tongue into my mouth, and at the same time he fondled my breasts over my blouse. I didn't kiss him back, but that didn't seem to matter. I was helpless to do anything about it. I remember him saying to the boys something like, 'You can have a good time with her tonight, she's an easy target.' Eventually, he left and went back to work. I slumped farther down to the ground, barely sitting up.

Now it was just Kelly and me with the two boys from our table. I had heard of one of them; he lived next door to a friend of mine and she really liked him. He was called Gerry, and it was easy to see that he was into heavy metal. He had the look: shoulder-length hair, lank and greasy; a denim jacket covered in heavy metal band patches; and blue jeans with a wide, black studded belt. He had seemed OK when I was chatting to him earlier on at the table. I had never heard of the other boy before that night. His name was Randall, and to me, he looked like your typical American. He wore a baseball jacket, which had a purple body and yellow sleeves, and short-ankle cowboy boots. I remember thinking the jacket was really cool – and that it was the only appealing aspect of him. At the café he had been very quiet, observing but not contributing. I wasn't contributing much either, but it was how he sat there: he seemed shifty and distant, with us but not *with* us. There was nothing warm or kind about him; he was not flirty at all. I learned that night that both of the boys had been living in London for two years while their fathers worked as diplomats.

They decided it was time to go. The boys lifted me up and walked me to the street. Without them, I couldn't have made the short journey – my legs were still rubbery and I couldn't balance on my own. Kelly followed along. One of the boys hailed a black taxi to take us back to her mother's empty flat. At first the taxi driver was reluctant to take us – he could see how drunk I was. He said he didn't want me to throw up in his cab, but he didn't object too strongly and so the boys talked him into it.

Many times over the years, I've wondered about that taxi driver. Why didn't he intervene? If he had, perhaps he could have changed the whole course of events that was to follow. He could clearly see the state I was in and what was going on in the back seat. Didn't he have a mother, sister, aunt or daughter? Surely he must have sensed the real danger I was in – he seemed to be more concerned about making sure I didn't throw up in his taxi. He told the boys to open the windows to give me fresh air. Other than that, he did as much as possible to ignore the scene reflected back to him in his mirror. What did he tell himself to justify his silence? Because in that silence there was complicity; he was, in a very real sense, the only adult in that car. It was a full taxi, but I was alone.

I sat on the back seat between Gerry and Randall. Kelly sat on a folding chair, opposite. As we got nearer to the flat, Gerry asked me for money to pay for the taxi. But I was unable to talk or give any response at all so he shoved his hands in my pockets, looking for money. He didn't find any, but fumbling around in my pockets must have given him other ideas. The assault began right there. Unbuttoning my jeans, he slid one hand inside of my knickers while he attempted to unclasp my bra with the other. As I tried to tell him to stop, I couldn't get the words out. I tried to push his hands away but he carried on, laughing the whole time, as if we were having fun. I don't know what Kelly and the other boy were doing; I was too concerned with my situation to notice. One thing was clear: I was completely vulnerable.

CHAPTER TWO

FORTY-FOUR BOWS

We arrived at Kelly's place. It was in an old block of flats in a section of North London called Hampstead Suburb Garden. One of the boys paid the fare, and they half-dragged, half-carried me out of the taxi, with each of them supporting me on either side. The flat was on the fourth floor and there was no lift. They indelicately pulled me up the concrete stairs and I felt every step as my legs bumped into them. One of the boys asked Kelly for the keys to unlock the door. Once inside, they took me into her mum's room, the first on the left. They took Kelly into her room across the hall.

I'll never really know how it was for Kelly. She was definitely less drunk than me. Even as we were arriving at the flat, it still looked like she was having fun. But after the boys took her to the room on the right, we didn't see each other or speak again until morning. And we never spoke about that night, so I can't accurately convey what happened to her or if she knew what was happening to me.

They placed me on the floor of the bedroom. It was a wooden floor with a red, blue and cream-coloured Persian rug. Gerry began taking off my clothes that were covered in vomit. He was not gentle in the process. First he pulled off my shoes, socks and jeans. He then wasted no time in removing my top. I remember him commenting on my hairy underarms and laughing at me. Randall was sitting on the bed, watching us, silently. When Gerry reached around to undo my bra, I became scared and realised they weren't going to put me to bed to sleep it off: they wanted more from me.

I realised in that moment that I was lying on a rug, nearly naked and completely drunk, in a room with two boys I didn't know, and one of them was doing whatever he wanted to me while the other looked on. To make matters worse, apart from Kelly, no one – none of my family or friends – knew where I was.

Gerry pulled off my bra and groped my breasts. There was urgency in his rough movements. He said to no one in particular that my breasts were big. He then felt up the rest of my body and put his fingers inside me. I was struggling against him, but he was too strong. He took my hand and held it over his crotch; I could feel his erection. The panic and terror rose inside me. I kicked my legs and swung my arms, trying to get him off me. I screamed as loud as I could, begging them not to do anything to me. Randall bolted off the bed, shoving Gerry out of the way. He straddled me and put his hands tight around my neck, pressing his thumbs hard into the base of my throat. Sheer terror shot through my body. He shouted at me to shut up while banging my head repeatedly against the floor. It felt like he was squeezing the life out of me. I was getting dizzier by the moment; I couldn't catch my breath. Everything was getting darker. I wanted to scream, but I had no breath and I thought I might lose consciousness.

Randall spat in my face and brought his face close to mine, all the while screaming and swearing at me to shut up. He then punched me in the face, quickly stood and kicked me with his boots, hard, between the legs. I felt the pain of his blows, but what really struck me was the look in his eyes. It was clear to me that he was dangerous and capable of killing.

Seeing that I'd got the message, Randall got up and returned to sitting on the bed. Gerry got back on top of me, pushing my shoulder against the floor while he undid his trousers. I could feel the heavy weight of his stomach on me, his studded belt stuck to the skin on my thighs; his jeans were only halfway down. As he entered me I experienced a pain like fire. I remember watching beads of sweat form on his forehead, roll down his face and then fly off onto my own face as he moved back and forth. They were disgusting – and I couldn't avoid them. I carried on watching the drops of his sweat, forming, rolling and flying, seemingly in slow motion, while he raped me. His breathing was so heavy and his head so close to me that I could feel his greasy hair flap in my face. His breath reeked of cigarettes. I could also smell his body odour, which was strong and stale, like he hadn't bathed or changed his T-shirt in days.

All the while, I heard people in the communal garden having a party. I could smell their barbecue coming through the open window in the bedroom. Adults were chatting and children playing the whole time he was on top of me. Rather than fight him off, a futile move, I wondered what they were having to eat. In those surreal moments of putting my attention outside the room I felt myself float right out of my body, and all of a sudden, I was looking down at the scene on the floor as if it were happening to someone else. But then I sank back into my body again where the pain and smells competed for my attention.

Gerry kept pushing into me, sweating on me, blowing his putrid breath at me. But then I noticed there was a border of wallpaper around the room at the top of the walls. It had pink and grey bows. I counted them over and over again, ignoring Gerry. Each wall section had eleven bows; there were four walls in the room: forty-four bows in total.

Before I even realised that Gerry had got off me, Randall straddled himself on top of me. He pushed one hand down on my shoulder and leaned close to my face. He said nothing as he looked me square in the eye and reached his other hand into his jacket pocket. I heard him click a button and then I saw it: he had a flick knife. He put the shiny, cold blade against my throat and told me again, 'Be quiet or I will kill you.' I knew he meant it; I never said another word after that.

* * *

The next thing I knew, I was awake with a jolt: it was morning. Naked but no longer on the floor, I was in the bed, and Kelly, fully clothed, lay beside me. She was wearing a load of bangles on her arm, and when she turned over, they jangled. I mistook the sound of her bangles for keys in the door – I thought that the boys were coming back.

When I tried to get out of bed, the pain was excruciating and seemed to come from all parts of my body. I felt as if I had been kicked and punched everywhere. Slowly I made my way to the bathroom and studied myself in the light. I was covered in blood, vomit, semen and excrement; I had cigarette burn marks on my legs and breasts. There were tear wounds to my vagina and anus. Around my right wrist and right ankle there were red marks. At first I didn't know what they were, but later I saw that there were tights tied around the pipes of the radiator. Yet it seemed Kelly hadn't been touched at all. To see myself in this way and to feel the physical pain was overwhelming, but all I wanted to do was wash it all away, so I ran a very hot bath and placed my battered body gingerly in the tub. Despite my injuries I wasn't capable at that point of feeling or thinking anything; I just wanted to get clean.

As I lay there in the hot water, loud confusion running

through my head, one thought stood alone, clear as a cloudless sky: my childhood was over.

For many years after that night, my memories of what happened after Randall held the blade to my throat and threatened my life were fragmented, difficult to piece together and distant to non-existent. It was too extreme, too violent for me to understand, let alone contemplate or review in my head. It's clear now that I was deeply affected by what those boys did to me. Keeping most of the memories locked away helped me, to some degree, cope with day-to-day life. And I was scared that Randall would kill me if I spoke of it to anyone. From time to time, a memory would bubble up and would instantly transport me back to that room, on that floor, reliving another aspect of the assault. But I quickly pushed the memories aside; they had no place in my life and I couldn't yet wrap my head around them.

How could I know that there would be several more assaults and that it would be many more years until I could be steady enough to examine the details of all that took place that night? How could I know that years later, in the process of helping women who were also victims of violence, I would begin my journey of discovery, of coming to understand not only what happened to me, but what happens to women all over the world? How could I know that one day, it was going to be OK for me, that there would also be tremendous beauty in my life? I couldn't. So, for a long time, those few details were all that I could consciously access. And really, I didn't want to access more.

CHAPTER THREE

NUMBING OUT

Kelly and I spent the morning tidying up the flat. We decided not to tell anyone about our night because we weren't supposed to be there and we had been drinking. But we said virtually nothing else about what had happened the night before, and tried to carry on chatting as normal, like two girls that had just had a sleepover. I went home in the afternoon and never said a word about it to my family. It happened on a Saturday night; I got back home on the Sunday afternoon and did the usual things that I can't even remember now. On Monday, I got up and went to school. It was another morning, another day in the life, normal.

I don't remember making a conscious decision to numb out, but numb out I did. When Kelly and I got back to school, we didn't talk about Saturday night, just as we had promised each other; we just did our typical school stuff. Except that things weren't normal for me anymore. I felt profoundly changed yet I was unable to understand or articulate why; I had shut out the vast majority of what happened that quickly. In time, and it didn't take long, I no longer recognised myself. I felt like I was a ghost of who I used to be. On the outside, I still looked the same, at least for the time being, but the changes taking place inside me were turning me into a different person. I managed to hide my injuries under my clothes; no one had any idea what was going on underneath them, and gradually over time the cuts and bruises faded. Going to the toilet was hard, as it stung every time I peed, but I soon got used to that.

In one sense, I had 'successfully' worked well with my mind to block out what memories I had from that night, but it came at a price. Slowly, yet steadily, I retreated deeper into myself and became quieter, more withdrawn, more aloof. Easy-going moments and spontaneous laughter drifted away. In their place compulsions and phobias developed and expanded, which were mainly to do with keeping me clean and safe. All the while, even as I saw them happening, I couldn't understand why I was doing them or where they came from – I was that detached.

I felt worthless, totally degraded and completely empty, as if I were renting my own body: I wasn't at home in it, I hated myself and I wanted to die. The assault was all my fault, I believed. I felt ashamed and guilty, but most of all, I felt dirty and contaminated. To combat those feelings, I would spend ages in the bath with bleach and household cleaning products such as Brillo pads, scrubbing my skin until it was raw. But it never felt clean, *I* never felt clean. I did that for years.

I disliked myself so much and felt so worthless that I was convinced I was a complete waste of space. What was my purpose in life? I couldn't see one worth living for. I became angry and hostile towards my family, who must have been baffled by the sudden and continual changes in me. My mum told me that she and my father could see I was disturbed and they were so worried, but I wouldn't respond to their questions, so there was nothing they could do. On top of that, I stopped having physical contact with friends and family because I was afraid I would contaminate them. But I never said a word to any of them about that fear.

Sleep was hard; despite being tired it took ages to fall asleep, and when I did I would wake up feeling panicked, but not sure what by.

Not surprisingly, I fell behind at school – my focus just wasn't there anymore. My work suffered, and I went from being a conscientious student with good marks to a poor student who didn't care at all. My taste in clothes shifted. I refused to wear anything that was remotely fitted; now only baggy clothes covered my body. The less people noticed me, the better I felt. I retreated further and further into myself, becoming increasingly quieter, particularly at home. Eventually, with the exception of a few fights and some sarcastic comments, I had no real conversations with my family. My silence lasted for almost three years.

The confusion I harboured towards these dark feelings made me feel out of control; I tried to stop them, but I didn't know how to. I don't remember making a conscious decision to monitor what I was eating, but I soon discovered that it was one of the few things I could control. Slowly, I ate less and less, experimenting with how little food I could survive on every day. Most days, I existed on black coffee, an apple and chewing gum.

One day at school, Angelika, who lived next door to Gerry, told me that he had asked her to give me a message. The mere mention of his name gave me shivers. The message was that I owed him money for the taxi from that night, and he wanted it back. She asked me what he meant, but I didn't know what to say. Dissatisfied with my lack of an answer, she asked Kelly, who said that we went out with Gerry and Randall, they took us back to her mother's flat, and I went off with the two of them, leaving her in her room.

A few days later, I saw Gerry on my way home from school. The way he looked at me was truly terrifying. It immediately brought to mind how Randall had threatened to kill me. Angelika told me that Gerry was bragging about a great night he'd had with me; he said that I'd got a bit drunk, taken him back to Kelly's empty flat and let him do whatever he wanted to me. He said we'd had a threesome. I couldn't believe my ears – his cruelty continued beyond the night of the assault.

People at school started to talk about it and they assumed I had enjoyed my time with Gerry and Randall. Very quickly, I developed a reputation for being easy. Unfortunately, this false reputation spread quickly, and soon it seemed that everyone at school believed the rumours. If I'd tried to dispel them, I would have had to talk about what really happened that night, and I was not going to do that. As much as I hated what was being said about me, it was the lesser of two evils.

I remember one of my friends sitting down and asking me exactly what happened that night. She seemed genuinely concerned so I made her swear not to tell a soul. I told her as much as I remembered. She told me explicitly that I had been raped and that I was in shock. I had difficulty taking in what she was saying and also struggled to say the word. However, what she said stayed with me and the word 'rape' kept going round and round in my head. Had I been raped? I really wasn't sure anymore but I didn't speak with anyone else about it, and my friend, keeping her word, never said anything either.

Despite how I felt about myself, I still wanted to be a normal girl and do normal things as much as possible. The rape didn't stop me from going out to parties, and there were parties almost every Saturday night. My friends and I would go to a phone box so that we could make our plans without any parents overhearing us. We'd call people from school that we'd heard knew about parties. After a few calls, we would find a party, get the address and 'gatecrash' it. In other words, we'd turn up even if we didn't know the people throwing the party and we weren't invited. These parties took place in houses where the parents were away, sometimes for a weekend, sometimes just for dinner. Most times, impromptu bashes were crammed with young people, loud music, a full bar and drugs. Many times, we had to leave quickly because the parents were coming home soon or the police had been called and were on their way.

By now I was rebelling at home a lot, especially during the weekends. My parents would tell me what time to come home, but I would ignore them and return whenever I pleased. One morning when I arrived home, my mother confronted me; she was so angry. She asked what was going on, saying that I was putting myself in danger and anything could happen to me. Inside, I was shouting back at her that it already had happened, but nothing came out of my mouth.

The rumours about my reputation soon spread beyond the scope of the school. Because of my reputation, and despite my baggy clothes, I received a lot of attention from boys at the parties we crashed. Often I found myself alone in a room with one of them; we would start kissing, and when they wanted to take it further, I would just give in and let them. I was scared that if I fought back in any way, they would respond violently and hurt me. Luckily for me, boys of that age, thirteen to fifteen, were only interested in foreplay. Still, I ended up doing things I'd rather not have done.

And so my reputation worsened, both in and out of school. I found myself living up to the name that I had wrongly been accused of. I believed, very strongly, that what had happened the night of the rape was my own fault, that I had brought it on myself due to my behaviour and that I was bad because I had lied to my parents, staying in my friend's flat when they believed I was safely tucked up at her grandmother's. As far as I was concerned I'd deserved what had happened to me.

Things continued to get worse, and I can't remember the exact trigger – I think I had an argument with my mum over doing the dishes – but whatever it was tipped me over the edge. I hated my life, hated myself and believed it would be better for me and everyone else if I weren't here anymore. So I went to mum's cupboard, where she kept her medication, grabbed several containers and took as many pills as I could swallow, washing each handful down with large gulps of water.

Afterwards I went up to my room. Lying on my bed, I thought about what I had just done and questioned whether I really wanted to die. Yes, there was all the pain and confusion that drove me to take those pills, but there was also a part of me that desperately wanted to speak to my parents about what had been done to me. However I could never find the courage or the words. Since my mum had been ill, I had always worried about saying anything to her that would upset her because I thought it could make her worse. As a result, I often kept my feelings bottled, worried about the impact on her. I also had a deep sense that if I told anyone about what had happened, I would be in trouble – and possibly even get killed.

So on 29 July 1979, I wrote in my diary for what I thought would be the last time: 'Everything goes wrong with me. I'm a complete failure. No one likes me. I've got no friends at school. My family hates me. What else can go wrong with my life? My life is not worth living. No one likes me. I feel so depressed. Cried last night after terrible nightmares. Had argument with Mum. Well, I won't have any more arguments because I've taken twenty pills of Ativan. Hope they kill me before Mum finds they have gone. I'll most probably go to hell.'

For some reason, soon after writing those words I went downstairs to my mum's room. She took one look at me and knew I had taken something. As panic rose in her voice she kept on asking me over and over, 'What have you taken? What have you done?' But I refused to answer. She shouted for someone to call an ambulance and rushed me to the kitchen, where she made up a salty solution to induce vomiting. I drank it all. I remember getting in the ambulance, but I soon fell unconscious. I've no recollection of arriving at the hospital or getting my stomach pumped.

When I opened my eyes, I couldn't believe I was still alive. My thoughts of worthlessness and feelings of failure just deepened even more. My God, I couldn't even kill myself!

The ambulance had brought me to Edgware Hospital in Middlesex to get my stomach pumped. I spent fifteen days there until I was transferred to a psychiatric unit for children called the Mildred Creak Unit (MCU), part of Great Ormond Street Hospital, because they thought I was at risk of overdosing again. The psychiatrist who had seen me on admission had written in her notes that I was seriously depressed and had symptoms of depressive disorder, insomnia, anorexia, psychomotor retardation, guilt and lethargy.

My first visitors were the ambulance men, who came to check that I was OK, which was sweet. But one of the nurses shouted at me and told me I was selfish. I didn't say anything back to her out loud, but in my mind I told her that I agreed. Was I making my parents suffer intentionally because I myself was suffering? It hadn't occurred to me before that moment.

I thought my time in the psychiatric unit would be brief, maybe a few days at most. In fact I ended up spending eight weeks in there.

CHAPTER FOUR

THE UNIT

The Mildred Creak Unit is a psychiatric ward for children between the ages of seven and fifteen. The entrance to the MCU is on a side building, separate from the main Great Ormond Street Hospital entrance. Its location often made me feel like they were trying to keep us out of sight. The ward, up on the fifth level, was designed to look like a flat so that it didn't feel overly clinical. Here the nurses wore their own street clothes and we called them by their first names. We had daily, closely supervised excursions to nearby Russell Square or Regent's Park. With the exception of those outings, and to attend school in the basement of the building, I lived my entire life for eight weeks on the fifth level.

There were roughly fifteen of us living on the ward; the number varied as kids were admitted and discharged. We shared five bedrooms between us. I shared one with a girl named Jane, who was suffering from depression and anorexia. She also swallowed safety pins. I'm not sure why, but I felt very protective towards her.

All of us were appointed a 'key worker', a nurse who focused specifically on a particular patient. Mine was called Alexa. She was nice enough, but I rarely spoke to her and usually responded by shrugging my shoulders if she asked me anything.

Despite how hard they tried to make us feel at ease and at home, I found it difficult to relax there. I felt constantly watched and scrutinised by the staff, and really, I was. Many times, I would quietly sneak up to the entrance of a room and would catch the staff talking about us in hushed tones. It only added to the feeling of being under a microscope. I was lonely there; I missed my family, my room and all things familiar to me. I couldn't believe I had ended up in a psychiatric ward – I knew how dark I felt inside, but in a very short span of time, I had lost sight of why.

I remained silent a lot of the time. The staff, beyond Alexa, tried constantly to connect with me and to get me to speak, but their efforts only made me more determined to remain silent. I would talk with the other children, but only when the nurses weren't around. One of the oldest on the ward, I liked the younger children, who often came to me for comfort or just to play.

Just as I'd forgotten why I felt dark inside, I had also forgotten why I wasn't speaking about what had happened to me. I had completely blocked out the death threat from Randall – I just knew it was very important for me to stay quiet. However, inside my head, I was shouting many words, responding to so many questions within the confines of my mind, but I couldn't make my mouth move to get the words out. I was frustrated, angry and hostile a lot of the time.

Occasionally, when I felt very overwhelmed and sad, I would sidle up to Alexa and just sit next to her without speaking or hold her hand on the way to the park; it was the only way I could communicate with her besides shrugging my shoulders. I hoped she would guess what had happened to me or hear the thoughts in my head.

And yet, for all their efforts to connect with me, no one ever asked if anything had happened to me. Instead, they focused on my continued refusal to eat most of the time, and would weigh me every morning to check whether I had lost or gained weight. I found ways to control that too: my roommate, Jane, showed me how to trick them by drinking lots of water before getting weighed and not peeing until afterwards, or by putting stones from the park in my dressing gown pockets, and leaning off the scales. All the while I never got caught. They would come to my room every morning before breakfast with my pills (antidepressants) and watch me swallow them.

Alexa would sit with me at mealtimes. If I didn't eat, and I rarely would, she would keep me at the table after everyone else had finished. She would do all she could to get me to eat – even try to spoon-feed me like a baby, forcing it into my mouth, but I would just spit it out. I actually enjoyed the control of restricting my food intake. It became a distraction to everything else I felt inside, and I think there was also a part of me that took pleasure in making people worry about me. Again, I hoped they would guess that something bad must have happened to me, because I wasn't able to tell them myself. But they never guessed and the cause of my condition was never addressed.

There were moments of levity. One of the male nurses had taught me how to play backgammon and I became a compulsive competitor, playing with him as much as possible and anyone else I could coax. I taught the game to as many people as I could, just to give myself more opportunities to play. Learning that game was the only real thing of value that I took away from my time there, and I still love playing it today.

I wasn't allowed any visitors, and the only time I saw my family was when they came every Wednesday for family therapy with the psychiatrist on the ward. This wasn't the first time I had met this psychiatrist: when I was eleven, I had been admitted to Great Ormond Street Hospital for nine days after I'd had what they'd called a 'possible convulsive episode' brought on by my worry and anxiety about my mum's health. He'd been my attending physician. From his prior history with me and these Wednesday sessions, he concluded that the whole family was disturbed and my condition almost certainly psychological. In other words, it didn't occur to him that something else, beyond worry for Mum, had happened to me.

So here I was with him again, two years later, and he kept going with the same theme from before, that my overdose was due to my difficulty in the direct and open expression of my feelings, especially those of a painful or aggressive nature, because of the unresolved conflict at home.

Mum told him I had been depressed for several weeks and that I'd lock myself in my room a lot. When I did come out, I'd argue with my brothers and sisters. But I wouldn't say anything in our family sessions. Looking back, I can see that the doctor tried to engage with me by making me angry, but it never worked. His tactics were clearly challenging to my parents, especially my mum, who was often in tears. I resented and despised those sessions so much, I'm sure the doctor could see how I felt.

He used to say to me: 'It's a pity you can't talk to me, as I don't know what you're thinking or what's wrong and I can't do anything about it.' Even though part of me wanted to make people worry about me, another part felt guilty for what I was putting my family through: it just compounded how bad I felt about myself.

Although the doctor couldn't get me to actively engage in the sessions, they were often very emotional for me nonetheless. Many times after the sessions, when she could see I'd been crying, Alexa would ask what was making me so tearful. I knew what, but I would just ask to be left alone and go to my room.

They would use the promise of letting me go home for the

weekend as blackmail to get me to eat. If I lost any more weight, I wouldn't be allowed out. But if my weight stayed the same or if I put weight on, I could go. As it turned out, I was only allowed to go home for a couple of weekends just before the end of my eight weeks in the unit, so the incentive had no effect on my eating, my desire to gain weight or my overall wellbeing. To me the control was more important than anything else.

After a few weeks on the ward I started going to the hospital school. The school wasn't just for kids from the MCU, but for all kids recovering in Great Ormond Street Hospital. It was very obvious what the other children were there to recover from – they wore plaster casts for broken limbs or had drip stands or bandages of some sort – but we from the MCU had no such outer signs of our wounds. I felt that when we all walked in, they knew which ward we'd come from: we were the mad children.

Even while I was at the school, which was off the ward and completely free of medical staff, I still refused to speak to the teachers and remained fiercely independent, not allowing them to help me in any way. In turn they reported back to the ward that I disliked being helped, was very cut-off and hostile, had a rigid manner and that I rarely spoke or smiled.

* * *

Slowly a pattern of daily routine started to emerge: get up, get weighed, avoid eating and talking, attend school lessons down in a basement in the main hospital, walk to the local park in the afternoon, ignore all the staff as much as I could, resist all efforts to encourage me to eat and then go to bed. It felt like a prison, and I wondered what I had done so wrong to be there – I was convinced I was being punished for taking an overdose. Even our exercise yard, up on the roof of the building, reminded me of a prison, being enclosed by a large, metal cage. They didn't trust that we wouldn't try and jump off the building, probably with good reason.

The feeling of imprisonment was particularly strong one day. All of us kids and a few of the staff were up on the roof for our daily dose of exercise. One of the patients, Clive, who was always causing trouble, managed to snatch the keys from one of the nurses. He threw them through the cage and out onto the street below, which meant we were all locked out on the roof, with no way to get back to the ward. Many hours later, a spare key was found and we were freed, so to speak. It was like a mini prison revolt. Part of me did find it funny, watching the staff panic, but it also perfectly illustrated how I felt living there: trapped in a cage.

Clive also caused trouble on the ward. He would smash plates, run around the ward screaming, lock himself in his room and vandalise the ward by breaking whatever he could. He once took a carving knife from the kitchen and threatened one of the male nurses with it. Sometimes, when he was shouting and screaming, it would take three or four nurses to subdue and control him. They would carry him away by his arms and legs, and then hours later he would return a much calmer and quieter version of his earlier self. To see him get so worked up was frightening and I think it affected all of us on the ward, but we didn't speak about it – it was a strange kind of normal.

While in the MCU I had my fourteenth birthday, and it was the most miserable birthday I have ever experienced. All day long I kept thinking of all my friends at school who were just living their lives, relatively carefree, while I was locked up. I despised myself and couldn't find anything positive to like about me.

When I look back to that time, I wonder why nobody ever asked me the right questions. Surely they could see I was traumatised, couldn't they? Then again, the doctor thought that my situation was simply a continuation of what he'd seen in me years before. So, in the absence of any other traumatic events they knew of, they diagnosed me a troubled adolescent with eating disorders, and that was where their focus remained, keeping me medicated on amitriptyline for depression and encouraging me to eat.

After eight weeks in the psychiatric ward, I was allowed to go back home. They released me because I'd put on weight and was now 40kg (compared to the 35kg I weighed when admitted). After weeks of defiance against the staff, my desire to go home was greater than my desire to continue to fight, but I wasn't really any better because nothing at the core of the issue had been addressed.

In his concluding notes about my inpatient stay, the psychiatrist wrote that he felt I had 'tendencies towards a rather depressive personality' and that there had been little change in my behaviour and mood while a patient. I still remained 'a worry of further overdosing given the still-existing family stresses'.

When I returned to school, no one asked me what had happened or where I had been, and that was just as well because I certainly wasn't going to talk about it. But I must have appeared like a ghost of the person they knew before I went to hospital. At first it was a shock to be surrounded by so many people again after being locked away, but I slowly got back into the routines of life. All the while, the numbness continued.

CHAPTER FIVE

COMING HOME

After eight weeks in the MCU, it was clear that virtually nothing had changed. My food intake was just enough to keep me alive, my confusion about myself and my life was just as deep, and my overall behaviour just as destructive. Actually, it got even more so. I'd barely been speaking at the unit, and that continued at home. But now there was a change: I found it hard to be civil at all and the slightest thing would set me off. I became very angry and hostile. If I did speak with anyone at home, it was only in the form of sarcasm. The screaming and fighting that used to be confined to my head had found its way out of my mouth and my family was taking the full force of it.

And yet, despite all that, I really wanted to share with my mum what had happened to me; I still wanted to be understood. Many times, I would go into her room when she was resting, as her neck and back issues were still making her weak, intending to tell her my story, but the words wouldn't come. I would just stand there in the doorway and she would ask me, 'What's wrong?' But I couldn't speak, so I would turn and leave.

I spent a lot of time by myself in my bedroom, listening to David Bowie. His music seemed to be one of the only things that could get into me. I especially loved 'Space Oddity' as, just like Major Tom, I felt like I had cut off all communication and wanted to float away into space and be alone. I would leave my room only if I had to, for meals or to use the bathroom. Mum had found out that I'd started smoking and she told me to smoke only at home. I never knew why: I think she thought maybe I wouldn't bother if I wasn't with my friends, but she was wrong.

Despite the fact that it was illegal in England at the time to sell cigarettes to anyone under sixteen, the man working in the ice-cream van outside school would sell them to me. I used my lunch money and skipped eating. The cigarettes helped curb the hunger, although by then I was used to barely eating anyway. Really, I just liked smoking. What I could buy from the ice-cream man wasn't limited to cigarettes; he would also sell me dope. And he wasn't my only source. If he wasn't around, there were dealers in the underpass between the two buildings of our school. Scoring was easy.

Most days after school, I could be found hanging out of

my bedroom window, smoking a joint to numb out whatever I was feeling, listening to Bowie. We lived in an art deco house in Hendon and I shared the top floor with my older sister, Rachael. Because my mum's bad back made going up and down stairs difficult, we were usually left undisturbed. But if Mum or someone else did come up to our floor, I had a lock on my door, which I put to good use.

I'm now deeply ashamed to admit this, but a few times I stole money from my mum's purse and from the till at my dad's shop in order to pay for drugs. To justify this, I told myself that I was doing what was necessary for a weekend of partying, but part of me also hoped they would discover what I was doing, somehow connect the dots and figure out what had happened to me: I wanted my bad behaviour to speak for me. It was a cry for help and another example of how conflicted and confused I felt.

Things continued to slip at school. I just couldn't focus and I had stopped caring. Before the rape, I'd loved school, but now I was juggling a lot of emotions inside me and found little to no motivation for my studies. Mostly I just felt like there was a black cloud following me that I couldn't understand, shift or shake.

I dreaded being at school, not only because I had lost interest in my studies, but also because I was paranoid that people would find out I'd been in the unit and had tried to kill myself. And so I just kept my head down and stayed within my circle of friends, which, as I attended an all-girls school, were mainly girls. When I was with them, I tried as best I could to act normal. Thankfully, no one asked me where I'd been.

In time, I forgot nearly all the events from that night, but I couldn't shut out the feelings that refused to be shut out or sealed away. Now I hated myself and couldn't believe that I was so inept that I couldn't even manage to end my own life. I had no self-worth and believed myself to be stupid and useless; I could see no purpose for my life.

Weekdays were hard work and time moved slowly, but I was still partying hard at the weekends. We always had parties or a club to go to but, no matter where we went, my reputation for being easy preceded me and followed me around.

My self-image was so low that I didn't care about my body anymore. All the respect I'd had for it was gone. I was alive and functioning, but found it hard to express and feel many emotions; it was as if I were on autopilot, just going through the motions.

My parents worried about me and tried so many times to help me. We continued to see the psychiatrist from the hospital for a few years, but I still wouldn't say a word to him so we stopped the sessions. Mum took me to see a few other counsellors and psychotherapists, but I refused to speak to any of them, too. Because of my silence, there wasn't much for them to work with and none of the sessions amounted to anything.

It was only a matter of time until a broad array of drugs was introduced into my world and my weekend party routine.

My chemical intake now included uppers, downers, LSD, cocaine and speed. I took them whenever I could get my hands on them, welcoming anything that helped me to block out any and all feelings that dared to surface. The numbness was what I wanted, yet on some level, I knew it wasn't helping me. It was easy to get drugs from other people at parties or friends, or I saved my pocket money and bought from the dealer outside school.

I had no problem getting together with boys, who obviously only went with me for what they could get sexually, and I let them do to me whatever they wanted. It was easier than resisting and possibly getting hurt – at least that's what I thought would happen if I protested, if I didn't deliver.

It only took a bit more time, but now the rumours were true: I would have sex with anyone who tried it on with me. I had no regard for myself and didn't care about contraception, relying on the boy to use something or pull out. But I couldn't do it sober; I had to be stoned or have a drink or two first. I can't imagine it was very enjoyable for the boys because I wasn't really present during sex. There's also a chance that they didn't really care. I had learned how to switch off to what was going on with my body and leave it, much as I'd done the night I was attacked. The difference? I was consenting to engage in sex. But the result, my strong desire and ability to leave my body, remained the same.

Sometimes I did not consent.

CHAPTER SIX

ANOTHER NIGHT

I belonged to a Jewish youth group called the B'nai B'rith Youth Organisation (BBYO) when I was fifteen, which consisted of Jewish kids aged twelve to eighteen. I had a lot of friends who belonged to the Stanmore group, so I joined too – I think my parents were happy to see me doing a social activity (other than weekend parties) and meeting new kids.

Through BBYO, I became friendly with some kids in a group from Luton, a town about 30 miles north of London. One of the boys from that group, Lewis, stood tall and skinny with a full head of red, curly hair. At one of the meetings he asked me to go out with him and another couple the following weekend for something to eat. By this time my parents had stopped giving me pocket money in an effort to prevent me going out, but it didn't stop me. I told Lewis I didn't have any money and he said that was OK, he'd pay for me.

They picked me up at my house and the four of us drove to an Indian restaurant not far away. At the end of the meal, Lewis looked at the bill, divided it into four and told each of us how much we had to pay. At this I panicked – had he forgotten that he'd said he would pay for me? I felt flustered, blurting out that I must have dropped my purse. We all looked for it, but of course we couldn't find it. Begrudgingly, he paid for my dinner.

On leaving the restaurant we split up into couples. We agreed to go for walks and that we'd meet at the car in an hour. Lewis took my hand and we set off in one direction while the other couple headed off in the opposite direction. We hadn't walked far when we came to a quiet, dead-end street around the back of some shops. There were no other people around, just big rubbish bins. He stopped, pushed me up against a brick wall and kissed me. It was horrible; he rammed his tongue into my mouth so far that I could hardly breathe. I tried to push him off, but he wouldn't stop. He licked my face, lips and neck as though he were eating me.

He stopped for a moment and smiled at me. I thought: Oh, thank God, he's going to let me go. But then he kissed me again and kept me pinned against the wall. I could feel the hard bricks on the back of my head as he continued to push against me, worried that I'd cut my head. It was still hard to breathe. Shoving his hands under my top, he grabbed my breasts, and I felt afraid by the change in him. He then pulled up my jumper and undid my bra, exposing my breasts. I could hear voices nearby and worried that somebody would come by and see us. But Lewis didn't care. As he bit hard into my breast, I felt a shot of pain. He then bit hard into my lip and whispered in my ear that he knew I wanted him and he'd heard that I liked it rough. I was crying and told him to stop, but he ignored me and my tears.

He pulled my short skirt up over my hips and ripped my knickers off. I kept telling him, 'No, please stop,' but he just carried on. Oblivious to my objections, he kept saying over and over that I wanted him and that I liked it. Then it got much worse. Putting a forearm to my throat and his hand up over my face, he pushed me firmly up against the wall and kicked my legs apart. With my face turned to the side, I could feel the bricks digging into my cheek, scratching it. I couldn't move. With the other hand he must have managed to get his pants down. He raped me up against the wall. As he pushed against me, the rough bricks continued to scratch my skin along the back of my body. I dug my fingernails into the wall to feel something else.

Again, I left my body. I sat on top of one of the big bins across the alley and watched the scene, as if it were all happening to some other defenceless girl.

When he had finished, his aggressive behaviour immediately evaporated. He even helped me get dressed. I couldn't put my knickers back on because they were ripped so I stuffed them in my bag. 'Told you that you would like it,' he said to me, and gave me a kiss on the cheek. But I was numb – I just wanted to get dressed and get home. Once I had my clothes back in their proper places, he again took my hand and walked me back to the car, where we met the other couple. During the drive to my house, the other two joked and said something like, 'Did you have a good time?' But I said nothing, my mind somewhere else. I felt so self-conscious of the fact that I didn't have any underwear on. They kept talking, but I didn't hear any of it.

The car stopped at my house and I didn't say a word – I just got out and headed straight in the door. A few days later, Lewis called and asked me to go out with him again, but I said no and told him never to call me again. Mystified, he asked why. I hung up on him and I never heard from him again. Fortunately, our BBYO group rarely met with his group, and when we did see each other again, he ignored me.

At the time I thought it was just bad sex. It would take me many years to see it for what it was.

CHAPTER SEVEN

OXFORD STREET

My sixteenth birthday came and went, and my behaviour grew worse. By now my parents didn't know what to do with me, so my rebelliousness continued uncurtailed. If they told me to stay in, I would go out; if they said I could go out but to be home by ten o'clock, I would reappear at midnight. I was rude and obstinate to them, often fighting and arguing back.

One night, my dad must have had enough of my defiance, and he locked the front door so I couldn't sneak in late without waking them up. But when I got home and found the front door locked, I just went round to the garden and slept in the shed. My parents were angry and shouted at me, which I just ignored.

One evening, it all got too much – I just wanted to be

away from everybody and everything. It wasn't anything I'd planned, it just happened. After dinner, I walked out the door straight to the park near our house and sat there for a while, still not knowing what to do with myself. Then I walked and walked through the night, all the way to Oxford Street in the West End, but it was too busy with creepy men who made slimy comments to me. I felt unsafe there so I walked back to my park and slept on a bench, under the overhang of a building that had public toilets in it.

I tried to sleep, but couldn't. It was too cold and I was too lonely and scared. Besides, I had another problem: I was wearing a jumpsuit, and in order to pee, I had no choice but to take the whole thing down. I dared not go behind a bush and I was too scared to go into the public toilets, thinking a man might be in there or would follow me in. So rather than take that chance, I just sat on the bench in the park and peed through my clothes. Of course the wet only added to the cold, and I must have smelled terrible. The night seemed endless.

Finally, the sun came up. Sleepily I walked to Golders Green, to a common area near the high street where I would sometimes hang out with friends. I saw two of my friends, who came rushing up to me; they were so pleased to see me. They told me that everyone had been looking for me and that they were worried. But I wasn't ready to go home and I felt hungry, so we went to McDonald's and got some food. Afterwards my friends called my parents, who collected me and took me back home.

My parents looked exhausted and concerned. When they asked me why I had run off, I didn't answer them. Again, I hoped they would guess. And again, they didn't. My sisters just looked at me without really saying much, but I felt they were annoyed with me and my rebellious behaviour.

I had spent a night away, but nothing had changed.

CHAPTER EIGHT

AND ANOTHER…

Turning sixteen opened up a new social frontier for me: clubbing. It became a weekend ritual and there were so many clubs to choose from. Our favourite place for Sunday nights was Busby's on Tottenham Court Road in the West End of London. Sundays were full of North London Jewish kids, roughly the same age.

It seemed every girl fancied a guy called Richard, and we saw him there every weekend: good-looking, popular and a bit of a character. Like all the other girls, I felt strongly attracted to him. One night, he came over and spoke to me. He then led me up to the fire exits of the club, where it was dark and away from everyone else. I was happy to go with him. We kissed and fondled each other over our clothes for a while before going back down to join our friends. He was a good kisser and I was excited that he liked me – until I found out that he and his friend were playing a game to see how many girls they could get off with in one night. I was just a number.

Despite the game he played that night he was still very charming, and over the following weeks at the club we talked more and more. It was hard to stay mad at him – and I didn't. Many times, we went back up to the fire exits to kiss and feel each other up. It never went beyond that and I liked doing it.

Richard worked in a clothes shop called Hobbs, and it was clear that he had a lot of really nice clothes. He talked about a suede T-shirt that he didn't want anymore, and said that I could come round to his place to collect it. Then he phoned me and arranged to pick me up and take me back to his house. My family teased me; they could see I liked him and they were excited for me. It was a light moment among so many dark times.

And so Richard picked me up as planned and took me back to his house. He mentioned casually that his mum wasn't home, and led me upstairs to his bedroom. We sat on the edge of his bed and after just a moment of talking, he started to kiss my neck and ears. Then he kissed me on the mouth and I responded. It was really nice. But the next thing I knew, he'd pushed me back onto the bed and got on top of me. He quickly lifted my shirt up and then pulled my jeans down. He was moving so fast; he only pulled my jeans off from one leg and then slid my knickers off the same leg. 'No, I don't want to,' I said. But he didn't listen. I pushed at him, but he had his weight against me and I couldn't move. He put all of his fingers roughly inside my vagina and, at the same time, his thumb inside my anus. I felt a shot of pain and confusion: what was he doing? How could he think I liked it?

Somehow he'd managed to get his own jeans down while keeping me pinned. My feet were still on the floor. He stood up and I kicked at him, telling him, 'No, stop!' But he still didn't listen. He kicked my legs wider apart, quickly got back down on top of me, covered my mouth and face with his palm, and pushed my head back towards the headboard. I couldn't move my head and found it hard to breathe; his palm was directly over my nose and mouth. Then he thrust inside me. There was nothing I could do to stop him – I just focused on getting air and numbing out from what he was doing to me.

Then it happened again. As he was thrusting into me, I left my body and watched the scene as if standing behind him. It was all so clear: I felt nothing, I just watched.

Then he pulled out of me and ejaculated on my stomach and all over my shirt. He handed me a towel and said, 'I'll order you a taxi.' The wait was surreal; he acted like everything was fine and chatted with me as if nothing had happened. In my confusion, I acted the same and chatted back. After all, that was just sex, right? But part of me knew that what I'd just experienced could not be normal or typical.

When I got home, straight away my family asked me if I'd had a nice time, but I went up to my room without saying a word. I felt numb. It had happened to me again and I couldn't cry or feel anything. Would this continue for the rest of my life?

I saw Richard at the club several times after that. At first, I could at least talk to him, but in time I found myself completely unable to even be near him, let alone speak to him. So I chose to ignore him, and eventually we never spoke again.

CHAPTER NINE

THE NOTE

Mum always warned me about how I should be careful around men, that they could take advantage of me, especially with how I was behaving. Inside my head, I was shouting out to her, 'It's already happened!' But I couldn't get the words to come out of my mouth. I hadn't had a real conversation with my mum, one that didn't involve shouting, in almost two years.

One night, my neighbour over the road threw a party. She was a bit wild and her parents were away for the weekend. My mum didn't want me to go, but of course I didn't listen to her and went out anyway. As if it wasn't bad enough, I didn't return until the next morning.

When I got home, Mum was right there, waiting for me. I could see that she'd been up all night. She was so angry:

shouting at me, reading me the riot act, telling me how worried she was about me. Something had to change or I'd get hurt one day, she told me.

I refused to react and remained emotionless while she shouted at me. She tried shaking me, but still got nothing out of me. Even when she hugged me, I just stood there. My mum's confusion was obvious: I could see that I'd pushed her and my dad to their limits and that they didn't know what to do next. They were desperate for a solution to the unsolvable puzzle I'd become.

My sisters were nowhere to be seen but my dad, who had been standing silently next to my mum, told her to stop shouting; I ran up to my room, slamming the door closed, and threw myself on my bed. As I lay there, I thought, my parents are desperate for a change, but so am I. What can I do? I so wanted to find my voice, but I was too scared to share – the death threat from years before still had me by the throat. Then it hit me: I may not be able to say the words out loud, but I can still write them down. That night, I wrote down all of the details that I could remember of that night. It wasn't a lot, but it was enough to clearly convey that I'd been assaulted. I left the note on my pillow before I went to school, knowing Mum would find it and read it.

My stomach churned all day at school. I couldn't hear a thing the teachers said. The anxiety and worry I felt about going home was almost unbearable, but I also felt relieved: Mum and Dad would finally understand what had so radically changed me over the last three years.

After school, I went right home, straight up to my room – and waited. After what seemed like a long time, both of my parents came up to my room and asked me if what I'd written was true. 'Yes, all of it,' I said. My dad was particularly upset and wanted us to report it to the police, but I begged him not to. I told him I was scared the boys would carry out their threat of killing me if I told anyone, especially the police. Mum's reaction was very different: she seemed to be dazed, in shock, and she remained very quiet, strangely distant. Her reaction, or lack of one, left a strong impression on me. It would take many years for me to understand her conspicuous silence.

My parents called Kelly's mum to speak to her about it. Her mum relayed Kelly's words: she denied it had happened how I said. She admitted to both of us getting drunk and staying over at her mum's empty flat, but said that the boys just took us home. They were nice boys and they would never do what I was accusing them of, she added. Looking back, it's true that Kelly didn't know the extent of what had happened to me, but the hard part was that she accused me of lying and didn't back me up at all.

I couldn't believe what I was hearing. It had taken me three years to finally tell my parents, and then I was accused of lying, of making it up. I cried and cried, and said it was true, that I wasn't making it up, that it did happen how I said.

Dad continued to insist we report the boys to the police, but my mum's silence led me, incorrectly, to believe that maybe she too thought I had made it up. Ultimately, we didn't report it. That night in London was not spoken of again for many years.

I just plummeted deeper and deeper into my blackness at that point. The last three years had been very difficult, but this was the lowest I had ever felt in my life. I couldn't understand why my friend would lie about it, and now I felt concern for what she might say about me to everyone at school. Was this really happening?

As if it wasn't bad enough before that call, going to school afterwards became even more of a struggle. Kelly told people about what I had 'made up' about that night. My friends didn't really speak to me about it. Still, the rumours spread quickly. Because I already had such a bad name for being easy, no one believed me. I felt so alone in it all.

Things at home got even worse than before. I hated them all and didn't want anything to do with them, so I just carried on acting out and hurting them with any chance I got. I felt my sisters were getting more and more annoyed and confused by me.

Contrary in every way, I continued to constantly challenge my parents. My mum gave me another lecture, this time about the dangers of drugs and getting involved with them. I shouted back at her that I was already doing them, as were most of my friends. To my surprise and horror, she called all of my friends' parents – as well as the school – to pass on that information.

All of my friends got into so much trouble. They were

angry with me and confused as to why I'd tell my parents about what we were doing. A girl named Gina was my best friend at the time – her father beat her with a belt. All of them were grounded. Convinced they would hate me, I dreaded facing them all at school – I felt so responsible.

I would go to school, but leave first thing after registration and hang around the park, smoking dope. Or I'd go to the shopping centre until it was time to go home. Wherever I went, I went alone. Most people at school thought I was a troublemaker and didn't want much to do with me, and so my feelings of isolation grew.

My O Level exams were coming up soon, but I had no motivation to study for them; I just didn't care anymore about myself or my life. I took them, but didn't pass many of them. Feeling as I did, I left school at sixteen with just a handful of bad grades.

My parents wanted to get me away from my friends, who they thought were bad influences. Their solution to that dilemma caught me off guard: they thought it would be a good idea if I were to spend a year in Israel, far from all the troubles in England. It would give me a clean start somewhere, they thought. I come from a Jewish family and both of my parents spent time in Israel. It was something they could easily arrange, it was affordable and it would connect me more to my cultural heritage. I was so lonely at that point, so exhausted, that I felt I had nothing to lose. And so I agreed.

CHAPTER TEN

KIBBUTZ

For many years after that first assault in London, I didn't remember the specific dates of any events in my life. Not only did I not want to remember most of what happened, I was also disconnected from the calendar; there were no personal landmark days that I cared to store in my mind or on a calendar, to later reflect upon. Only weekends stood out, but even those weren't worth noting. The days all blended together into a grey haze. But 21 September 1982 stands out in my mind – that date was different.

Along with about twenty others, I set out from Heathrow Airport to Israel for a year. It offered a new start, the chance to leave the pain of the last three years behind. I'd just turned seventeen in August and I thought maybe, just maybe, this year would be different, better.

I remember feeling nervous and excited. The people in our group weren't complete strangers; I had met them all a few times at preparation meetings over the previous weeks. We were all pretty close in age although I was the youngest one. Some of them had been to Israel before, but this was my first time. It was also, with the exception of the stay in hospital, my first time away from home without my family.

Our year was to be split between two locations. The first six months were on the Kibbutz HaSolelim, which is in the north of Israel, about ten miles west of Nazareth. We spent the next six months in Ashkelon, a village on the Mediterranean coast, in the south of Israel. It's about ten miles from the northern border with Gaza. The two places were very different from each other in many ways, not just geographically.

As far as kibbutzim are concerned, HaSolelim wasn't very big – the community consisted of about five hundred people. The majority of the population were Israelis, but there were also South Africans, Americans and, of course, British, too. Volunteers made up about 20 per cent of the total population. The kibbutz grew cotton, bred chickens and, in a departure from the usual rural elements, ran a plastics factory. We were required to work for our keep. I worked in the dining room in return for food, laundry, lodgings and a small amount of money per week.

I shared a room with two other girls in the volunteers' block. The rooms were basic: our three single beds and a paraffin shower. That shower was like nothing I'd seen before or since. There was a water tank attached to the wall with a heating tray underneath it. Before taking a shower, we had to ignite the paraffin in the tray to heat the water. It was dodgy! A virtual light show of flames poured out from under the tray every time we used it, but it worked and we never burned the place down. Our small windows afforded the most amazing views of the hills in Galilee – they were just endless green. It was a beautiful, serene setting.

Life there was simple and straightforward. It was filled with hard work and routine, but I really took to it. Work started early, at 6am, but our shifts were finished by lunchtime and we had the rest of the day off. Usually I spent those afternoons relaxing with the rest of the group by the pool. It felt so good to be in warm sunshine, and we were getting to know each other better every day.

There were a couple of full-time members who looked after our group of volunteers, and each of us was also assigned kibbutz 'parents'. My parents were kind, lovely people and I got along with them really well. My kibbutz mum had a big, warm personality. She was very motherly with me and I liked it. My kibbutz dad didn't say too much, but he was also very kind. Every few weeks I'd go over to their home for a meal with their family, so we didn't have a whole lot of interaction. Still, I knew that they were there for me if I needed anything.

Throughout our year away, our group went on many arranged tours and we saw a lot of the country. It was beautiful. Best of all, it was different and new.

I threw myself into kibbutz life and became determined to understand Hebrew while I was living there, speaking it as much as possible with the kibbutzniks. I had a basic knowledge of Hebrew, having learned some fundamental reading and writing in Sunday school, but I had never been that interested or eager to learn more. That changed while I was in Israel: I embraced my culture as never before.

My parents were right: it was good, really good, to get away. I missed my family, but I didn't miss the mess I had left behind. It was a profound relief that no one in my new circle knew anything about what had happened to me, and I tried to keep it that way.

I still battled with the dark feelings inside me, but I continued to push them down, ignoring them. All my new experiences were a good distraction and I could see no reason to let any of those memories spoil my time away. They had no place in my new life, I believed.

I felt safe and protected living there, away from everything: it was a bit like living in a bubble. For the first time in years I started to relax. But I still wasn't eating well, and my low weight continued to prevent me from menstruating. I think my habit of not eating was strong, and I still had no appetite. Also, I got seven packets of cigarettes per week free from the kibbutz shop, so those, along with the usual suspects (black coffee, an apple and chewing gum), were my main diet.

I found that as long as you did your work, people accepted you. No one cared what you wore or, within reason, what you did. I loved the laid-back way of life there. We worked hard but we enjoyed ourselves too, celebrating whenever possible. The festivals on the Jewish calendar were often a good reason for a party, and I was lucky enough to witness a kibbutz wedding while there: the couple were driven to the ceremony by a tractor, the groom in his shorts with no shoes on. You wouldn't see that in London!

There was an old air raid shelter that had been converted to a bar and we would spend a lot of nights there, drinking and socialising. One of the weekly highlights was 'film night' in the dining room. None of the homes had televisions, so this was our only chance to get our viewing fix. It was also another opportunity for the young people in the community to get together – I loved it.

Communication with the outside world was minimal. There were no phones in the homes; the only phone on the kibbutz was in a small room off the main dining hall. When a call came in, it would often take a lot of running around to find the person the caller was trying to reach. I received calls from my parents and we had short conversations. Those were our first real conversations in years. It was nice and I was surprised by how much I missed them.

The teenagers who lived on the kibbutz year-round had their own block of living quarters, away from their parents and the other adults. They grew marijuana among the fields so it was readily available. Often I would smoke with them and listen to music after work. I laughed to myself, thinking about my mum, who had wanted to get me away from the drug scene – and here I'd landed straight into another one.

Despite the fact that so many aspects of my life were going well, I still had no respect for my body and continued to have sex with anyone who tried it on. The Israelis had a perception of foreign women being easy and I guess I didn't disappoint. Just like the boys at home, they didn't seem to notice or care that I wasn't present when they were with me. And as before, I often left my body during sex.

The first six months came to an end and our group moved down to Ashkelon. I was torn: I loved living on the kibbutz and didn't want to leave, but after discussing it with one of the leaders, I decided to give it a try. We agreed that if I hated Ashkelon, I could move back. That made the move much easier. At that point in my life, I couldn't imagine returning to the UK – I even had thoughts of moving to Israel permanently.

CHAPTER ELEVEN

ASHKELON

The housing arrangement in Ashkelon differed from the kibbutz. All of the volunteers lived in a large block of flats called The Hostel. But The Hostel wasn't just for volunteers; we lived among new immigrants and Israeli families, too. Among the wide array of people living there, some of them were clearly fighting their own demons. I remember a Russian man, often drunk, who would sing out of his window, and an American Vietnam veteran who we heard, many times, shouting at his wife and children along the corridors.

Our volunteer posts were spread throughout the town. You couldn't just fall out of your room and walk sleepily up a path to work; getting there involved using buses and mixing with the general population again. I wasn't living in the bubble any more.

I had my own room on the second floor, and avoided taking the lift because cockroaches would fly out of it whenever the doors opened. It made the stairs an attractive alternative.

I didn't feel as safe here as I'd felt on the kibbutz, because by the end of my six months on the kibbutz, I knew most of the people living there. It was intimate. This felt like starting over again – and it was. As on the kibbutz, each of us volunteers was assigned a leader to look after us. Mine was nice, but we were much more independent here. So I, like everyone else, rarely interacted with my leader. Yet despite all the differences, some things were very similar. Together, we lived in The Hostel, went to work, socialised, partied after work and received a small wage. The beach was about a twenty-minute walk across the sand dunes and I spent a lot of weekends there. I loved the beach; it was a beach like you'd never find in England.

And just like on the kibbutz, it was easy to score dope when I wanted to. There was no grass grown in Ashkelon, but the dealers were known to us and made drops frequently at The Hostel. One of the dealers had no legs and was confined to a wheelchair; he kept his stash under his seat. His condition did nothing to slow his business.

The work I found in Ashkelon was really interesting to me. While at school I had enjoyed art and wanted to find a way to use it there in a work environment, so when I found Interaction, a company that used art projects to bring disparate communities (like Ashkenazi, Sephardi, new immigrants and Israeli Arabs) together, I knew I'd found the right place to work.

And how right I was. We made sculptures and murals which we raised using cement. 'Raising' involved painting images on layers of cement that we added to the wall, giving the images a 3-D effect. One of the first projects I worked on was at a primary school. We designed a Garden of Eden theme and the main focus was a long, raised snake sculpture in the centre of the playground. The children came from different religions and varied backgrounds, but they all worked together to build it. The instructors and children were broken up into groups and each group was given a space to paint a scene. In the end, we created something very colourful and beautiful. To celebrate the opening of our work, we arranged a party with a snake charmer and we invited all the locals. I loved seeing this. There was nothing political about it – the innocence and joy in these children really moved me. And I think many of the adults were moved, too. I really enjoyed my work and getting involved with all the different projects.

Getting to work on the bus was a bit of an adventure. To simply get on the bus, I had to fight off old ladies carrying their groceries from the market. If you didn't push back, you'd never get on! Once on the bus, we were all squished together, jam-packed in place. It could be equally challenging to get off the bus when my stop came.

Outside of work, my social life picked up where it had left off at the kibbutz. I continued to party and meet boys, and for the most part it was fun. But then something happened that made me wonder if my life would ever really change.

CHAPTER TWELVE

AND AGAIN

I had been living in Ashkelon for about three months when I started spending time with an Israeli guy called Noam. He was tall and skinny with a nice smile and a relaxed way about him. His family had emigrated from Morocco just before his birth here in Israel. A lot of local Israeli guys hung out around The Hostel and he was one of them. He was also one of my connections for weed. These guys thought that all foreign girls were easy. How did I know that? They didn't know that I could speak Hebrew. I would hear them talk about us – and it wasn't so nice.

Noam seemed different to me, kinder. We spent hours in my room, talking and listening to music. As I relaxed more, we became intimate and had sex a few times. Sometimes he'd spend the night in my bed with me. There were no red flags at this point; he acted respectfully and gave me no reason to feel cautious or guarded with him.

We had spent a day at the beach and were walking back to The Hostel when he stopped to kiss me. It was nice; I kissed him back. But then he held the back of my head and I felt it was too strong so I pulled away. Undeterred, he rubbed my breasts over my clothes and I told him, 'Stop, somebody might see!' That didn't stop him either. He rubbed my crotch over my clothes and again I told him to stop. He stopped, kind of laughed it off and we kept walking.

We got back to The Hostel and I asked him into my room. For a while, we just lay on the bed, talking. He turned over towards me and kissed me again; this time I told him I couldn't do anything because I had my period, which was true. He said it was OK, that he wouldn't do anything apart from touch me. Then he stuck his tongue in my ear and moved it around very fast and it made me feel sick. It wasn't nice anymore. Then he put his hands up my dress and inside my bra, pinching my nipples. It didn't feel good – it just hurt. Then he moved down to my pants and slid his fingers inside my underwear, and again I reminded him I had my period. It made no difference to him, and that surprised me; I thought he would listen to that statement with respect. But he kept going. He rubbed my clitoris and he kept asking me if it felt good: it didn't. I said nothing. He pulled my dress up so my body was exposed. Then he rubbed his hands very fast all over me. He pulled my breasts out of my bra, squeezing both of them hard, and sucked my nipples.

When he got on top of me I could feel his erection. He undid his trousers and said he wouldn't do anything; that he just wanted to rub it against me. Then he moved up and down, simulating sex, all the time asking me if it felt good: none of it did. He took my hand and put it on his penis, still inside his underwear, and made me rub it. Then, while on top of me, he took his penis out of his underwear and, holding onto it, rubbed himself against me. He pulled my underwear to the side and rubbed his penis against my vagina. All the while he kept asking me if it felt good. I just lay there and let him rub himself against me.

Then he started to get rougher, pinching my breasts even harder, biting them, biting my stomach and the inside of my thighs, rubbing his hands all over my thighs, scratching my legs and rubbing himself up and down on me with increasing speed. He kissed me hard with a fast-moving tongue, bit my neck and pulled my ponytail, forcing my head backwards. Moving down to my vagina, he rolled down my knickers and started to lick and bite my clitoris while squeezing my breasts. He licked and bit the inside of my thighs and pinched my bottom.

It was too much. I tried to push him off and I told him to stop, but he didn't. Relentless, his hands were all over me. He was so tall and heavy that I couldn't get him off. Then he pulled my pants down even more and inserted himself inside my vagina. I told him to stop – I was wearing a tampon – and that he was hurting me. With each thrust he pushed the tampon further and further up inside me. 'Stop it, you must stop it!' I repeated. But he replied, 'It feels good, doesn't it? You like it, don't you?'

After a while, he ejaculated inside me. He lay on top of me, and inside me, for a few minutes before he finally got up and dressed. I just lay there, not moving. Then he sat down next to me on the bed, stroked my cheek and hair, and kissed me on the lips. He said he couldn't help himself, that it was my fault for getting him excited. I felt disgusted, used and dirty again.

He lay on the bed with me for a while, trying to cuddle me, but I was out of my body again. About thirty minutes before, I had flown to the balcony of my room and watched the scene of my struggle from out there. After a bit longer, he left. I went straight to the bathroom to retrieve the tampon as I was worried he could have ruptured me internally; it took me a while to find the string.

I was seventeen years old and I'd been sexually assaulted four times. With the exception of the first assault in London, I thought it had all been just bad sex. It would take years for me to see the rapes clearly for what they were. My parents had sent me to Israel for a change, but from my perspective, nothing was changing. I had told them about the assault when I was thirteen and nothing had changed. Was this to be the rest of my life? What would it take to stop this terrible momentum?

CHAPTER THIRTEEN

STEVEN

There were groups of volunteers from all over the world arriving constantly at The Hostel and I became friendly with a lot of them. I thoroughly enjoyed meeting people from such different backgrounds, and it was a welcome contrast to life at home that I embraced fully.

Among the arrivals, I noticed two guys who had come out from Glasgow. Well, I noticed two, but one in particular really got my attention. He was called Steven and we would have short chats whenever we bumped into each other. I liked bumping into him. Steven was twenty (which seemed ancient to me at the time!) and had come over for a few months during his summer break from university. He had a job and a wage, but he didn't work very much, at least compared to most of us; however, that didn't mean he didn't get an international reputation to the contrary. A photograph of Steven cooking with a Moroccan woman in a local kitchen was published in Jewish newspapers all over the world, so his relatives in Glasgow and New York were so proud of the good, hard work he was doing.

About four weeks after the night with Noam, I was in my room, drawing, when I heard a knock at the door. I opened it to find Steven and his friend standing there. This was a very nice surprise. His friend said hello and quickly disappeared, leaving Steven there alone and looking pretty uncomfortable. I had heard that he liked me, but that he was too shy to approach me for anything more than a passing chat. Later on, I found out that his friend had fed him a few drinks to build up his courage before bringing him to my door and making a hasty exit.

From that night on, for the six weeks I had remaining in Ashkelon, we were virtually inseparable. We ate most of our meals together, went to the beach, saw movies and attended parties. The time with him was fun and easy.

Things were so different with Steven. Unlike my other sexual experiences, he was gentle. And even though he was after what he could get sexually, like most men I had met, he didn't hurt me or rush me. I felt safe with him, and straight away I knew I could trust him. Those were not feelings I was accustomed to. For the first time in my life, I could see a future with a man. I knew he would never harm me, even though I still couldn't work out why he wanted to be with me. He was cute and smart and kind, and he could be with anyone else. I noticed I wasn't leaving my body as much as I used to; I risked more of myself, and even though I still had to be stoned or a bit drunk to be intimate with him, I stayed increasingly present and more in my body each time we made love.

By the end of our six weeks together, I was totally in love with him. I believed that he was an angel, sent to save me. He stopped my life from going in a very different direction. He wanted to be with me despite the image I had of myself; he made me feel worthwhile again. I couldn't believe my luck that he wanted to be with me. I thought he would be like all the other guys I had met before, who would just take what they wanted, sexually, and leave.

Steven would be heading back home to Glasgow a few days before I would be leaving for London. Although I assumed I would never hear from him again, I so wanted to be wrong.

CHAPTER FOURTEEN

LOVE

After Steven left, the days in Ashkelon seemed unnaturally long. I missed him a lot. I was convinced I'd never hear from him again, but I was, much to my amazement, very wrong. Not only did I hear from him, but he and a friend of his stayed overnight in London at my parents' house on their way back to Scotland. My family liked him. When I got home a few days later, I found a note he'd left under my pillow. He called me on my first day home. Could it be that he actually liked me?

Despite all that, I couldn't fully accept his feelings for me. I was very excited, but also very suspicious. Once we met up again, he would surely change his mind about me. It was just a matter of time, I thought.

Within a few days of being back in London, we made

arrangements that I would stay with him for a weekend in Glasgow. He was a student at the time, studying for a degree in psychology, sharing a flat with another student. I felt so excited and nervous during the whole train ride north – it made an already long journey feel that much longer. When I arrived, he was there at the station to greet me. Initially, I felt a bit shy and awkward around him, but those feelings melted away quickly. We had a great weekend together and I loved being with him. It just seemed so natural, as if we had always known each other. He spent more time with me and didn't change his mind!

We soon fell into a pattern of travelling up and down the UK, visiting each other. About every two weeks, one of us would take the train or overnight bus to London or Glasgow. I made more trips north and was happy to do so; we had more privacy at his flat. Between visits, we would call and write to each other, and I waited impatiently for his letters to arrive. We were inseparable in Israel and that trend continued at home.

Although I travelled north more than he travelled south, I still had a busy schedule. I had enrolled in a beauty course at a private college soon after I got back home. It was a pretty intensive course, cramming two years of work into nine months. I didn't have many qualifications after leaving school and my options were limited, but I enjoyed my studies and they kept me busy during the week while I waited for my fortnightly visits.

I didn't really pick up with my old school friends. It seemed that a lot of them were still angry with me, and I felt like I had changed too much from my year away. Mostly, I didn't want to go back to my old habits.

Things at home were a bit easier, though. My family and I relaxed with each other; our time apart had clearly made a difference. Now we actually talked to each other, and although there were still disagreements, there was no more screaming. But I was still convinced that my mum didn't believe me. It kept me distant, no matter how much things were improving between us. I was also convinced that I had been raped because I was a bad person – although I couldn't figure out what I had done in this lifetime to deserve that, so I assumed it must be my karma from a previous, evil life.

I still felt so much shame and guilt. It was my fault for getting drunk and putting myself in a dangerous situation; I was stupid and naïve. After all this time, I still felt contaminated by it, still scrubbed my body with cleaning products and scouring pads. But none of that could remove the smell that I thought lingered on my body.

Steven still didn't know what had happened to me and I didn't want him to know. I assumed that if he knew, he would change his mind about me and would never want to see me again, as if the rape were a reflection of my character.

When we were together, I would question him over and over again: 'Why do you want to be with me? What do you see in me? Why do you love me?' I was grateful that he did, but I couldn't understand why. The image I had of myself was still so low – and so contrary to the one he held of me.

With Steven, so many things were very different. For the first time in my life, I began to enjoy sex. I didn't just lie there anymore, wishing it were over; I wasn't leaving my body. There were still a lot of things I didn't feel comfortable doing, but that didn't cause any problems. This man showed me patience and kindness that I'd never encountered with a sexual partner before.

Despite my efforts to keep the rape buried within me, the more I relaxed with him, the more my secret would surface through my actions – especially when we were in bed. There were times that, in an instant and for seemingly no reason, I would be overwhelmed with panic and would push him off me. At other times, his face would suddenly turn into Gerry's or Randall's and I'd burst into tears. As much as I tried, I couldn't perform oral sex on him: the fear and shame felt too great. It usually ended with him comforting me while I sobbed.

I worried that these emotional outbursts during sex would jeopardise our relationship and drive him away, but Steven remained supportive, steady and never complained. Again, I couldn't believe my luck. Part of me waited for the bubble to burst.

After being together for two years, Steven completed his psychology degree. This was his second degree (he also had a degree in computer science), and if he had found the funding,

I think he would've gone for a third! He decided, much to my approval, that he wanted to live in London to be near me and to start his career. He rented a room in a flat just up the road from me, in Hampstead Garden Suburb, and we saw each other as often as we could. Going up the road was a lot easier than going up to Glasgow – it was great!

There was just one downside to where he now lived. Whenever I passed a block of flats on the way to his place, I would experience strong panic. I knew those were the flats I'd been taken to that night, but the few details I remembered of what had happened were very fuzzy in my mind. I couldn't understand what was going on with me but I couldn't ignore what my body was telling me: fear and utter terror made me feel sick every time I passed by. It became too much and soon I avoided that route altogether.

One night, Steven and I went out to meet his cousin's new boyfriend at his flat. It turned out he lived in that same block of flats. His place was at a different end of the building, but that didn't stop the sheer panic I felt inside. I could hardly speak to any of them that night. The extent of the panic still confused me.

There was another confusing thing going on with me: the more I relaxed and felt safe with Steven, the more panic and fear came out in everyday life. I distrusted men and felt threatened around them, especially men I didn't know. I began acting with resentment, hostility and sarcasm towards them. For example, if a man walking towards me on the street looked at me, immediately I'd feel unsafe and would cross to the other side of the road. While out and about, I continuously looked over my shoulder and became obsessed with my safety. I avoided public transport if I could, especially at night. And for reasons I couldn't yet figure out I would never take a taxi – I just couldn't trust them. It got to the point that unless my friends could give me a lift, I wouldn't go out.

Whenever I got in a car, I would immediately lock all the doors. I saw potential threats and attacks everywhere. When I was out by myself I found it hard to relax. At night I couldn't walk outside by myself, not even to the bins at the end of the garden. I don't think people really understood what was going on inside me. I thought I was hiding my fears well, outwardly stoic despite the inward panic. I became hyper-vigilant about my security. Eventually, I found it nearly impossible to be around men, even in a professional capacity. I saw only female dentists, doctors or opticians.

And yet, despite all that was going on with me, Steven and I were growing closer. I spent several nights a week at his flat. Things carried on like that for a while. Eventually we decided to buy a flat of our own and move in together. We bought a two-bedroom flat down the hill from Alexandra Palace in Hornsey, North London. It was on a quiet road with good neighbours and I loved it. Our life together was something I'd only dreamed of, and Steven made all of that possible.

The feeling of being an imposter in my own life never left me, though. At any given time, I thought, Steven would come to his senses, change his mind and break it off with me. But he never did.

After about five years of going out, I decided to have 'the conversation' with Steven about the direction of our relationship. It seemed I'd stolen his thunder; he told me that he loved me and was about to ask me to marry him. He'd planned on taking me to a restaurant with a ring so he could propose, but I beat him to it!

Before formally asking me to marry him, he first went round to my parents' house and asked to speak to my dad, who was in bed with flu at the time. But neither of them would be deterred, and Steven asked Dad for his permission to marry me. My dad happily obliged. I think this says a lot about Steven: his actions were thoughtful, honourable and respectful. My love for him continued to grow.

With freshly given permission from my father, Steven proposed to me, right there, in my parents' house. Of course I accepted! We called Steven's mum in Glasgow to tell her the good news. She was very excited. The proposal was also a relief for my old-fashioned dad, who had been embarrassed that his daughter was living with her boyfriend. He'd often said to us that we should get married; that he was worried about what his friends would think of us, an unwed couple living together. Many times he offered to pay for our wedding, just to encourage us. Well, he no longer needed to worry about what his friends might think.

We got married on a very cold and snowy 20 November

1988 at my local synagogue in Hendon, North London, surrounded by all my friends and family. It was a very happy day, full of love and celebrating. We left the next morning for our honeymoon in Kenya, where we combined chilling at a beach resort in Malindi with a safari in Tsavo East, Tsavo West and Amboseli. To me, life couldn't get any better – or could it?

CHAPTER FIFTEEN

BEST REVENGE

From the outside, the only thing missing from our perfect life was children. But I made it very clear to Steven that I didn't want children and he seemed OK with that. Our two cats were our babies, or at least we spoiled them as if they were.

In my mind, having children would be like getting raped again, and I wouldn't put myself through that. Just thinking about it set off instant fear and panic within me. By this time, I felt secure enough about our relationship that I told Steven I had been raped when I was thirteen. He stayed very quiet when I told him, and just told me he was sorry and held me. We had talked a bit about having children, but now he understood my resistance and didn't want to push the subject.

Even if we ourselves didn't talk about it, people would ask the usual question that they do of newlyweds: 'When are we going to hear the patter of tiny feet?' I would just tell them flat out that I couldn't have children, and that usually stopped the conversation cold in its tracks. To me it was unbelievable, the number of people who asked that question. After a time, I found it hard to be polite towards them.

We settled into our daily life and it was lovely. Steven worked as a software programmer in the City of London and I worked as a beauty therapist in a salon in Hampstead. Most of the time I enjoyed it, but whenever I had any male clients, I immediately tensed up and refused to do more than a back massage on any of them. We offered full-body massages, but I couldn't yet be alone in a room with a man who didn't have his trousers on – even in a safe, professional environment like the salon.

At the risk of stating the obvious, winters in London are long and grey. To make them a bit easier, we would save up our annual leave and take long holidays. We travelled to the Gambia, Thailand and India, all for several weeks at a time. They were great holidays, full of sun and relaxation. Getting away from London and all the memories I had there provided me a real sense of relief, if only for the duration of a holiday.

It was exactly that kind of space and relaxation that allowed me to make a major shift in my thinking. It was November 1991 and we were enjoying the last day of a beautiful holiday in Thailand, on the island of Ko Phi Phi. While walking on an idyllic, tropical beach, Steven wondered out loud about starting a family. Is it something I'd want? Wouldn't it be great to share our lives and love with a child? His questions were so sincere; I felt no pressure coming from him. Perhaps out of habit, I answered with the usual: 'I can't do it, it feels like too much.'

But in that moment, walking by the sea in the warm sunshine, something happened that altered my life forever. I decided right there that yes, I wanted to have children. If I didn't, those who raped me would take away a huge part of my life. I refused to let that happen. Already they had taken enough of my life. In that moment, I declared to myself that my best revenge on those who assaulted me would be to lead a good and happy life. No longer would I allow the course of my life to be determined by what they had done to me. That moment, that declaration, started me on a journey of healing – and that journey included motherhood.

That wasn't the only big decision I made that day on the beach. If I were to become a mother, I'd need to get some help. I didn't know what that would look like, but I had to get over my fears of giving birth so we could start our family. It was time to turn and face that which I'd been running from for so long.

CHAPTER SIXTEEN

STEP ONE

We returned home and I immediately began the search to find a suitable counsellor. Of course, it had to be a woman – I couldn't trust a man. Fortunately, we lived very near an area of London called Crouch End, which goes by the nickname of 'Couch End' because of the abundance of counsellors working there.

The first therapist, a Freudian, hardly said a word and just allowed me to speak. I remember her making a comment about how interesting it was that my father and I had both experienced trauma at a similar age. (He survived the Holocaust – his story is very moving and I'll explore that in a later chapter.) When she did speak, she asked me all about my dreams. Perhaps it was interesting, but I couldn't work out how this was going to help me so I stopped seeing her after two sessions.

After that I went through several more therapists who left me feeling equally dissatisfied. I wondered if I'd ever find someone to help me get past my fears. In my mind, I pictured giving birth on a hospital bed in a room flooded with bright light, my legs up in stirrups, surrounded by male doctors, everything exposed, no dignity or respect, with all aspects of the process out of my control. That picture was enough to put me off for years. I wanted help with my new and fragile desire to have a child, and I had yet to find it.

It was time for a different approach. I thought back to when I'd returned from Israel in 1982 and seen a hypnotherapist, a kind man from Liverpool called Joe Keeton who specialised in past life regression. He would come to London every month and meet with a group, which included my mother, to explore past lives. The meetings were held in the homes of the group members, and every now and again they were held at my parents' home. Often the sessions went late into the night. My mother had got into hypnosis years before; it was the only treatment that had a massive, positive effect on her. She'd gone from being bedridden and full of pain to up and about without any medication. It allowed her to enjoy life again. So I joined the group when they came to my parents' house. I did so mostly because I wanted to learn about my past lives but also because I was curious about hypnosis.

Joe's philosophy was that certain issues from our past lives affected our present lives, but we have to work through the blocks of our present lives before we can get to any blocks from past lives. And therein was the problem: every time he hypnotised me and guided me towards the events of the night with the two boys, I'd end up screaming and trying to climb out of the chair, terrified. It seemed my screams were quite loud, which disturbed the people in the group, and it was a source of concern that the neighbours might hear and complain. We were about to give up when he suggested we try it one more time, but this time at his friend's house in the countryside near Leeds. Out there, I could make as much noise as necessary without concern. It worked in the sense that I didn't have to worry about the noise I made, and I did feel freer, but I still had the same reaction every time; it always ended with me screaming in panic.

It seemed like I'd never get past the blocks from this life. During one session, before putting me into a hypnotic state, Joe said he could see that there was tension between my mum and me. He was right; I told him that I thought she didn't believe I was raped. This caught my mother completely by surprise. She said it wasn't true and rushed over to console me. We hugged and she cried. Things felt a bit easier between us, but I found it unnatural to hug her and I imagine I must have come across as quite stiff. That moment with Mum, as nice as it was, didn't change my mind.

I liked hypnosis and could see it was helping me, but the sessions continued to end the same way every time so I decided to stop. Now that I'd seen several therapists without any real progress, I decided to give hypnosis another chance and went in search of a female hypnotherapist.

I found Vera Pfeiffer in Ealing, a London borough west of our flat. I remember feeling very nervous for our first appointment. Perhaps there was some safety in the group I'd just left. Regardless, Vera put me at ease the moment we met. She led me to a lovely studio in the garden behind her house. We sat down and I told her that I wanted help to get over being raped so that I could get pregnant and give birth without the panic I imagined. I wanted the whole experience to be joyful and free of fear. And I wanted to feel in control of it. 'No problem,' she said, and that relaxed me even more.

Vera practised psychotherapy with hypnosis very differently to Joc. Rather than taking me, while under hypnosis, immediately back to the assault, she guided me, also under hypnosis, to put the events of my life into a 'book'. At my own pace, I could go to the pages, the events of my life, and look at them from the outside as if they had happened to someone else. By looking at the events in the book, the emotional charge that accompanied these memories almost completely dissipated. I could look at what happened without screaming, without feeling the terror. Using this method, I relaxed enough for the contents from the vault in my mind, sealed so tightly for so many years, to slowly begin creeping under the door and into the light of day, into my conscious mind.

When we got to the scenario of the first rape, she asked me what I would do now to change things, how I would do it differently. For example, she wanted to know what I would change about the taxi ride back to the flat. While under hypnosis, I had the taxi driver kick the boys out and drive me back to my parents' house.

We had about ten sessions, going through lots of the different things that were done to me. For every situation, I changed what happened, under hypnosis, to neutralise the trauma. After each session, I could feel the tension and panic within me shrinking. The combination of seeing the events in a book combined with my ability to change the events and their outcomes allowed me to access many more memories than I ever had before.

During one session, I had what could be called a breakthrough. For a long time, I'd had an inexplicable fear of injections. Over the years I'd dealt with it by getting as few as possible, but sometimes the doctor would insist and I would squirm, forcing the nurses to hold me down while the GP administered the injection. For me, being held down only compounded the feeling of terror. So when I learned that I would need a number of blood tests and injections if I were to get pregnant, I got very anxious. Under hypnosis I saw, for the first time since the attack, that both Gerry and Randall had burnt me on my breasts, thighs and lower legs with their cigarettes. The sting of the doctor's needle felt just like getting burned with cigarettes. I was shocked by these memories that I could see so clearly for the first time in my life. Despite the dissipation of terror, the sessions were difficult and painful, but good. I also wondered and worried: were these memories real? After all, they had been discovered with hypnosis and I wasn't sure if I could trust them. Did those things happen? Did I make them up?

CHAPTER SEVENTEEN

MOTHERHOOD

Hypnotherapy was clearly helping me. As I looked at more events from my past, some phobias melted away. But I still had a difficult time around men, and because of that I did my research on hospitals before I became pregnant. I couldn't go to a regular National Health Service (NHS) hospital because they couldn't guarantee that no men would be present during the birth. Also, I wanted an environment as natural and relaxing as possible – not always a strength of some NHS hospitals.

I found the perfect place: the Hospital of St John & St Elizabeth in St John's Wood, where they ran a very small birth unit that felt personal and intimate. They completely understood my fears once I had explained where they stemmed from, and assigned me a female consultant who would guide me through it all. Straight away we agreed that there would be no men present throughout the entire process.

They were very forward-thinking, empowering women to use their natural instincts rather than drugs or medical interventions such as cutting, the use of forceps or the ventouse. Instead, they promoted an overall low-tech approach that included aromatherapy, reflexology, homeopathy, water pools and low lights. They offered yoga classes and counselling for expectant mothers. I would be given a room with a double bed and Steven would be able to stay with me for however long we wished. After meeting the staff and seeing the facilities, I knew this was the place where I would give birth. I was getting excited – and I wasn't even pregnant yet!

I had been off the pill for about a year when I missed my first period, so I did a home test. The result was positive (I checked the box several times to make sure) and showed it to Steven as soon as he came home from work. But I had no symptoms at all and didn't trust it, so we delayed any celebration. I then went to the pharmacy to get a more formal test done, and that result was positive too. OK, it seemed I *was* pregnant! But I was still not convinced: I didn't have morning sickness, I had no metallic taste in my mouth and my breasts weren't tender. I had none of the classic signs of a pregnant woman, so I convinced myself that they would soon tell me it was a phantom pregnancy and there was no baby. Over the years I'd developed a mentality of hoping for the best but expecting the worst.

I made an appointment to see my doctor and it was only during my first scan, when I saw the little heart beating, that I knew it was true. OK, I really am pregnant! From then on, I couldn't keep the smile off my face.

I had terrible nightmares while I was pregnant. Many times, I imagined that my baby would die inside me. My team at the hospital assured me that this was normal, and that even though they couldn't guarantee it wouldn't happen, it was very unlikely. I think I just couldn't believe my luck and thought it would soon run out. It didn't help that the hospital was located next door to where Gerry and Randall went to school, the American School of London. And yet it seemed the appropriate place to continue my best revenge plan; the fact that I would be giving birth next to their old school, that my lovely husband and I would be bringing a beautiful new life into this world, felt like sticking two fingers up at them.

In the prenatal yoga classes, I learned breath work and toning. These classes also helped me realise that I wasn't in my body and in fact I hadn't been for many years, as if my head wasn't attached to the rest of me. For so long I'd felt empty, like I was just renting an unfurnished house. When I breathed in during the classes, it felt as if my breath was filling my whole body, right down to my feet. I felt more connected to myself and grounded than any time I could remember. They taught us how to focus on the breath to help with the contractions, and to go with them rather than fight them. Every contraction I experienced would be one nearer to meeting my baby. The toning involved making deep sounds from the pit of my belly. I felt very self-conscious and a bit silly to start with, but was reassured that this too would help during the birth.

After an easy pregnancy health-wise, my baby, who was clearly in no hurry to go anywhere, decided to appear ten days late on 13 May 1993. The birth went relatively well. I had wanted to give birth in the birthing pool, but I threw up in it at the end stage and got out to give birth on land. I only used Entonox (gas and air) and controlled breathing for pain relief. Throughout my pregnancy, I had been listening to a hypnosis tape that Vera Pfeiffer made for me to help with my breathing, and I think it made a difference. The toning exercises also really paid off during the contractions. And oh, the sound I made – it even surprised me! I was quite shy and didn't think I'd be able to tone in front of everyone, but when the time came, nature took over and I found my voice.

Steven and the midwives were a great support, encouraging me the whole way. I felt safe and secure with them all. When it looked like the baby would come out soon, the midwives put me in a supported squat in order to get the most natural position – I was terrified of being torn. At one point, they told me they would have to do an episiotomy, and that was not something I wanted at all. To avoid being cut, I started pushing like all hell was let loose. After pushing for what seemed like an eternity, I told them that the baby was stuck, but they reassured me that they could see the head and encouraged me to touch it. My fingers met my baby's head and I felt a load of hair. It gave me what I needed. With a deep breath and a big push, our daughter Anna was born.

The rush of emotion I felt was unbelievable. It was, without a doubt, one of the most precious moments of my life. I felt as if my heart would explode with happiness and pride. Not only had I brought our daughter into this world, but I had also faced my fears and refused to be limited by what had happened to me. As I looked down at my beautiful baby with her abundant dark hair, I kissed the top of her head and wished her only good things and a happy, healthy life.

CHAPTER EIGHTEEN

MOVING ON

We'd brought our beautiful baby home and life was going great. We named Anna after Steven's grandma. In Hebrew, her name means 'favour' or 'full of grace' – and that she certainly was.

After talking with other new mums in my local National Childbirth Trust (NCT) group and the baby massage classes at the hospital, I quickly realised that in comparison to the experiences of others, Anna was an easy baby: she was very laid-back, relaxed and happy. I put it down to having a straightforward birth with no stitching, tearing or intervention. My natural, instinctive birthing powers kicked in and I felt I was in control. I never felt scared by the contraction pains; I knew they were only bringing me closer to meeting my baby. Instead I felt very empowered by it all and it shifted something inside me.

I totally loved motherhood – the easy birth and relaxed baby made it all easy to love. Just after the birth, while Anna was still attached to me, they'd put her onto my skin and she'd fed straight away. It was so natural – she knew what to do. I never had any feeding problems at all. She would cry, I would feed her and she would sleep.

We didn't experience any colic pains, she never cried through the night and we never had to drive her around in a car to get her to sleep, as some of my friends had to do. She was just so easy: she slept twice a day, fed with no problems and woke up only once a night.

My mum warned me that I might get the baby blues a few days after her birth, which she assured me would be normal, but they never arrived. I felt so content with life and any thoughts of being unsafe were fast becoming a distant memory. The usual haunting concerns seemed to melt away as all of my energy went into Anna. But there was one exception to the tide of safe, happy, maternal feelings and it surprised me. It arose when Steven changed Anna's nappies. When I saw a grown man around a naked, vulnerable female, fear and panic rose in me like a volcano. But just as quickly as it would rise, I would remind myself that this wasn't just any man, this was Steven, the lovely father of this beautiful girl. He was nothing but gentle and kind with her. Still, it showed me how much I wanted to protect her. I didn't tell Steven I had these fears and, of course, I let him carry on changing and bathing her: they were very sweet together.

I spent my days with other mums, with my family, or out seeing friends and going to baby groups such as swimming classes and baby massage. The changes in my day-to-day activities, my life, were huge and wonderful.

I was very fortunate as I was effectively my own boss, working as a freelance beauty therapist just before I had Anna. Together we made the decision that I would take time off to spend these special moments with her and I'm so grateful we could afford to.

My relationship with my parents was so much better, and they loved their time with Anna, but they'd had quite a scare a few weeks before. While I was giving birth, my mum had called the hospital to get any news about me and to find out how I was doing. She was told there was an emergency going on and they had to get off the phone immediately. Afterwards she became convinced that I was the emergency. When we called to tell her that Anna had been born, my parents were at my bedside very quickly, within thirty minutes. Mum looked sick with worry, and I discovered she had been pacing the floor at home all night, waiting for any news. She had already worried about me so much over the years that it broke my heart to hear that she'd had all that unfounded concern.

Once they got to the hospital and saw that Anna and I were OK, my mum and dad were instantly fine. There was something so magical in watching my parents hold their granddaughter for the first time. Seeing Dad with Anna in his arms, sleeping peacefully as he walked her around our room, was something so precious and especially so because I thought it was something that would never happen.

Life was beginning to feel really good, really settled, in ways I'd never known before. I threw myself into motherhood. To be the best mother I could possibly be was an integral part of my best revenge plan.

Everything was going swimmingly, but unfortunately there was an economic recession going on in London. I wasn't working and Steven's job was unsafe; he had already survived many rounds of redundancies. Later on in 1993, his father offered him a job in Glasgow in the family business, a factory making pre-stressed concrete lintels for the building trade, and after some serious thought he decided it would be the best option for our family.

I couldn't believe it: he wanted to take me away from the safe bubble of the world I had created. It brought all my fears to the surface. Again, I became concerned with emotional and physical security. Questions I'd not thought about in the months since Anna was born ran through my head. Where would we live? Would we be safe there? More importantly, who could I trust?

Our flat went on the market, and I harboured hopes that it would take ages to sell so I could prolong the move. To my horror, it sold really quickly, so when Anna was just six months old we moved up to Glasgow with all of our belongings and our two cats.

Just as quickly as our place sold, we found a house in a small cul-de-sac. It was great, but needed work done on it, so we lived with my in-laws for three months before we moved in.

For me it was hard. I felt ripped away from the life I had built up in London; there I was, starting over again in a new city far from home. It had taken many years and a lot of effort to create a life that I could move through – and that was gone with one move. The insecurity inside me grew and I could feel my resentment towards Steven building up.

On top of all the old fears coming back with a vengeance, something new, something I'd never experienced before, happened almost every night: I started to cry. I would wait until Steven was asleep and weep silently into my pillow. I didn't know why I was crying; the tears just leaked from my eyes. This went on for at least the first year in Glasgow. I'm not sure Steven had any idea what went on while he was sleeping. If he did, he never said anything.

Eventually, I'd cried enough. I decided that this was where I was living and I would have to make the best of it, despite missing my family and friends and longing to go back to the life I'd been torn away from. The first thing I did was join lots of baby groups – it was easier to be sociable with a baby. The best revenge was back in focus.

Within a year or so I felt more settled and was beginning to relax, despite still missing my old life. Things between Steven and me got easier and I let go of a lot of my initial resentment towards him. I accepted that this was my new life and I had to make the best of it, which I did.

When Anna was about eighteen months old, I decided it would be great to go back to work, but I didn't want to return to the world of beauty therapy or work as a make-up artist again. I felt there was something driving me to work with women, and as a result, I found myself volunteering at a local Women's Aid group in East Kilbride, South Lanarkshire. I worked a couple of shifts a week and they paid for Anna to go to nursery, which was on the way there. It all worked out really well.

Women's Aid is a remarkable non-profit organisation doing important work to help women in the UK who have been victims of domestic abuse. They offer a broad range of services designed to help women escape abusive home environments by providing counselling, legal advice, temporary refuge housing with a transition to more permanent housing (provided by local councils), childcare services and, most importantly, a safe place for women to rebuild their self-esteem, recover from whatever trauma they've experienced and set a course for a new life.

My training involved looking at the history of domestic abuse, the effects of it, and how little women were protected. It made me so angry to learn how badly women were treated and I felt the profound injustice of our imbalanced society.

To start with, my job was very general and I helped out in many areas. I worked in the advice centre, explaining all the services available to the women and guiding them towards those they would most benefit from. I also helped out at the refuge, filling in funding and housing applications, and took children on days out to theme parks, the safari park and the zoo. I loved the variety of the work. Most of all, I loved working with the women, watching them transform from when they first arrived at our advice centre to when they got permanent housing after receiving treatment at the refuge. It could take up to a year to get council housing, but that time was crucial for building emotional strength and setting practical aspects into motion. The women would come through the doors frightened, downtrodden and somewhat broken, and emerge much stronger, healthier, more self-assured versions of themselves. It was incredibly gratifying and very touching to see. Every day, I was amazed at the strength of the women who often left their homes abruptly with hardly any possessions and chose to start all over again.

I also found that I was able to listen to their stories and not be shocked by what I heard. I think that made it easier for the women to open up to me; they didn't have to worry about how I might react to some of the more violent or embarrassing aspects of their lives.

For many years I'd wanted to work at a Rape Crisis centre, but I couldn't have done it straight away – it would've been too much and I wasn't yet ready to help others. So I eased myself in at Women's Aid, working with victims of domestic violence for a few years until I felt ready to make the change. When the time felt right, I applied to be a volunteer at my local Rape Crisis centre in Glasgow.

Similarly to Women's Aid, we had to complete a training programme before we could work on the helplines or help the women face to face. I remember one day of training particularly well: the topic of discussion was the effects of rape on a woman. It hit me so hard to see the words on the flip chart; most of the symptoms listed were the same ones I'd dealt with the entire time since I was raped. And the list was long.

The list included self-blame, shame, suicide attempts, drug or alcohol misuse, low self-esteem, body image issues, early sexual activity, less safe sexual activity, involvement with the criminal justice service, anger, cutting oneself off from people and aggression. These were things that I knew well from first-hand experience. The only thing listed that I hadn't done was self-harming, but that's only because I was terrified of knives and being cut.

Other than that one exception, I identified with all of it so much that I couldn't ignore it anymore. Part of me knew that I had been raped, but I still had strong doubts because, with the exception of one friend at school and my father, no one believed me – at least that's what I thought at the time. I was shocked by this revelation, but also bolstered by the fact that I now had clear evidence that all the feelings I'd had for years didn't come out of nowhere: they were the result of being raped that night when I was thirteen. I couldn't ignore the facts in front of me now. But there was still a part of me that refused to believe it and constantly asked questions: why had it happened to me? What had I done wrong? But that part of me was finally, after all these years, taking more and more of a back seat. Yet I still didn't know how this newfound perspective would affect me.

Once I'd completed my training, I worked a few shifts per week on the helpline. The work itself was not hard for me, but getting to work was emotionally difficult because most of my shifts were at night, which meant driving and walking to the office by myself. I wasn't always able to park close to the centre, so many of those walks were long and terrifying. Despite the progress I'd made, for me walking alone at night was still very challenging. But once I was inside and on the phones, I forgot my journey there and focused on the women on the other end of the line.

Again, the work ignited the anger inside me. These women had been abused, assaulted and raped in so many different ways, often at the hands of men they knew, be it their partners, family members, neighbours or friends. Men had raped them because they chose to and this clear fact hit me deep in my gut.

I had so many questions that I couldn't find the answers to. What was the point or purpose to all this violence? Why do we hurt each other so much? How do so many men get away with it? How can the chain of violence, so often passed down the generations, be broken? I realised that while I was so angry with men, I was also angry at life!

CHAPTER NINETEEN

DISSOCIATION/ PTSD

That night in London with the two boys had been reclassified in my head: I'd been raped. There was now no doubt. And listening to the stories of all these women on the helpline made me continue to look at my own experiences. I could relate to so much of what they said, and understood their perspectives in a way that only someone with first-hand experience could. Now I knew why. But there was more: I realised that I'd been very promiscuous and had had a lot of meaningless sex. This was not a major revelation but pretty quickly, after listening to enough women describe the assaults they themselves had survived, a more significant revelation hit me: I'd been raped on three other occasions.

In my mind, those events had simply been bad sex. Steven showed me how different, how enjoyable, sex could be. But it was the stories of these women that made it clear that what had happened on those three occasions was not just bad sex: it was rape. The boy from the Luton BBYO group, who had taken me out to dinner and tried to make me pay after he had said I'd be his guest, raped me against the wall on that dead-end street. Richard, the good-looking boy from the club on Tottenham Court Road, raped me in his bedroom at his parents' house, and Noam had raped me in Ashkelon. Those three events stood out in my mind with crystal clarity. Despite that clarity, something else now confused me: why could I remember all the details of these lesser date rapes yet hardly recall any details from that night when I was thirteen?

During my training at Rape Crisis, I learned about dissociation, post-traumatic stress disorder (PTSD) and the corresponding symptoms, particularly after a woman has been raped. We learned that the symptoms may appear within a few months of the event but can sometimes take years. Another light bulb went on inside my mind, this time for the possibility that I'd had some kind of dissociation for all these years.

Although the training material covered several forms of dissociation, two in particular stood out. The first, dissociative amnesia, is characterised by an inability to recall important personal information that is especially stressful or traumatic. This form of amnesia is too comprehensive to be put down to ordinary forgetfulness and cannot be attributed to an organic disorder. I remembered some of what had happened with the boys that night in London, but I knew there was still a lot that

I could not yet recall. The second, depersonalisation disorder, is characterised by a recurrent feeling of leaving one's body: those suffering from it say that it's as if they are watching their own lives from a perspective outside their bodies. This was all too familiar.

Regarding PTSD, there are different types of symptoms: avoidance, negative changes in thinking, changes in emotional reactions and intrusive memories (which I didn't have yet, but they would come later). They all resonated with me.

While I didn't have distressing memories about the event, I did have emotional reactions to things that reminded me of it. For example, if I saw anyone wearing an American baseball jacket, I would panic. Or if I saw someone with long, greasy hair, I'd have the same reaction. Even hearing any mention on the radio of or reading anything in the paper about rape would set me off, too.

The more I thought about it, the more evidence of my condition came to light. I definitely avoided places when I lived in London – I went out of my way to avoid driving down the Finchley Road where it all started, or past the block of flats where it all happened. If I was a passenger and had no choice in the journey, I would look the other way and hold my breath until we had gone past the flats, all the while feeling very sick and panicky.

I had countless negative feelings about myself and often felt emotionally numb. While I didn't feel hopeless about the future, I often got scared by thoughts that the beautiful life I now had would all be taken away from me, that Steven and Anna would be killed in an accident in which only I would survive.

My memory was also really affected. It was as if, when cutting off the memories of the rape, I'd also cut off childhood memories. Whenever the family got together and reminisced about times when we were all younger, I honestly couldn't remember the things they talked about. I felt like I had lost large chunks of time from my childhood. Many childhood memories have never returned.

I particularly identified with what we learned regarding emotional reactions. Often irritable, I had angry outbursts and was hostile or sarcastic to any men who I thought were making any kind of come-on or even a compliment towards me. Always I was on my guard and scared of being attacked again. Above all else, for years safety remained a high priority. I still felt so much shame and guilt, believing it was my fault, and after all those years, I still hated my body. These were classic signs of PTSD – and there was more.

Unexpected noises startled me easily, and I was very jumpy when I heard a sound I didn't recognise or if someone surprised me from behind. Sometimes I had trouble concentrating and could lose hours, not really knowing what I had done in that time. I also used avoidance as a coping tool for any feelings I had, because I didn't want to appear weak or vulnerable. For many years, I thought that showing any emotion was a sign of weakness, even loving emotions. It took me a good many years and a lot of hard work to undo that perception.

Sleep was something that troubled me for years. It took me ages to get to sleep in the first place and when I finally did, I would wake several times in the night, sometimes mumbling and fighting an invisible enemy. I couldn't remember those night fights; Steven would tell me about them later. Often I felt tired in the morning and on edge for the rest of the day.

All these symptoms suggested to me that for years I had been living with PTSD, like a soldier who had been in combat. I learned that trauma, especially at a young age, shatters innocence and creates a loss of faith and meaning in the world; nothing feels safe or predictable and no place offers a safe retreat. I also learned that traumatic events can be too big for the mind and body to process, and due to their shocking and overwhelming nature don't get integrated or digested. And then the trauma takes on a life of its own, haunting the survivor and stopping him or her from leading a normal life – until it's treated.

I didn't just recognise most of the symptoms, I'd been living them too. I then realised it was because my body and psyche had been exposed to extreme violence, terror and fear. I'd experienced a helplessness that very few people ever feel at any age, let alone thirteen. This revelation completely changed the way I'd been viewing my entire life since that initial rape. It was unsettling, but vitally important. Now I had a better idea of what I was up against in my mind and in my body, where the echoes of shock still remained. What would I do with this new perspective on my life?

CHAPTER TWENTY

HOME BIRTH

When I was twenty-nine, Steven and I decided that it would be great to have another baby to add to our family. What better way to continue my best revenge, especially after the revelations I'd had about the events of my past? To me, it was a beautiful way.

But given what I knew about hospitals in Glasgow, there had to be a better place for giving birth. My perspective of hospitals was still the same: I feared it wouldn't be a supportive experience, and I had heard too many bad stories of medical interventions and things going wrong. More importantly, I couldn't find anywhere as forward thinking as the Hospital of St John & St Elizabeth in London.

Another perspective also remained intact: it still felt too overwhelming for me to have much contact with men, even in a professional capacity, but especially when giving birth. And no hospital in Glasgow would guarantee that men would not be present during the process. Nothing could compare to the experience of Anna's birth – or could it?

I decided the only option would be a home birth. After all, my experience at St John & St Elizabeth had been like a home birth in almost every way, except the 'home' part. I wanted to feel safe, not just for me but for my baby too. Having a child at home meant that I would only be attended to by midwives, and that kept any potential anxiety – and men – at bay.

It seemed like no time at all before I got a 'positive' reading on a home pregnancy test. My body was ready to go! The pregnancy was great – incident-free, just like my first one – and I loved being pregnant. For me it was always such a joyful time. I was still working part time at Women's Aid and got a good maternity package from them, which would, among other things, allow me to stay at home with my baby, Mimi, for longer – nine months, rather than the standard six months.

There weren't many home births carried out in Glasgow at that time so I was something of a novelty. Most of my friends and neighbours thought I was a bit crazy, but they didn't understand my fears surrounding men and feeling out of control. That was OK; I preferred being perceived as a bit crazy to risking any man being involved in the process.

When I told my doctor that I wanted a home birth, she supported my wishes but still arranged for the head of midwifery to come to my home, meet me, check out the potential setting for the birth and give her stamp of approval, so to speak. She did indeed visit, realised I was quite sane, saw that I had towels and hot water, and gave me the green light!

Like the first time, I did as much as I could to prepare myself for a natural birth: I listened to the pregnancy tapes that Vera Pfeiffer made to help me relax; got some homeopathic remedies for during and after the birth (like arnica powder, which I took every two hours to prevent bruising); made up a music playlist to relax and motivate me; bought aromatherapy oils to be rubbed into my back; and started drinking raspberry leaf tea, which is said to strengthen the uterus wall, shorten the second stage of labour and promote the creation of rich breast milk. And Steven brought home the all-important plastic sheeting from his work.

It was great, being supported by the eight community midwives. They were so excited because home births were rare at the time, and each of them urged me to go into labour on their shift, as if I could fulfil such a request! They would take turns coming to my house every few weeks to do check-ups and make sure everything was as it should be – they were a joy to work with.

Just as with Anna, I had an easy pregnancy with no complications. This time I had put on more weight than the first time round, but that was the only physical difference. I still managed to get to the gym and do all the classes I had done before I was pregnant, and I started going to yoga and swimming classes for mums to be. I wanted my body to be in the best shape possible for the big day – or days.

Around my due date, porters from the local hospital delivered all the things I'd need, including a tank of gas and air for pain relief, scissors, baby resuscitation equipment, absorbent pads and syringes. I looked into getting a birthing pool, but using it upstairs in my bedroom would have required some kind of constructive support, and it wouldn't have felt right using it in my front room downstairs (what if someone rang the doorbell while I was in the midst of giving birth?) so I scrapped the idea, as nice as it sounded.

Anna, who was now three, was very excited that she was going to be a big sister and every bit as eager as we were to meet the new arrival.

Having my baby at home was perfect for me. I had two midwives who were there only for this one delivery; they didn't have to disappear down a corridor to attend to someone else, supporting Steven and me through the birth was their only focus. It all felt incredibly right and I never worried about anything going wrong with the delivery.

Unlike Anna, this baby was in a hurry to enter into this world and I went into labour five days early. But just like with Anna, all the sound and breathing techniques I'd learned instinctively took over and my body knew exactly what to do. In fact, they brought me straight back into my body just like the last time, and made me realise that I don't spend much time in it. But this was not the moment to ponder such things, so I moved that thought aside for the time being and focused on my contractions.

It was all pretty straightforward: when the contractions began, I used my bath for some time to relax (I found the water so soothing), then went into my bedroom to give birth. And after eight hours of uncomplicated labour, Mimi arrived on 21 March 1996. It was an easy birth with no damage to my body, which was a huge relief. The midwives cleaned my baby and me, and helped me into bed after giving birth on the floor. I had a cup of tea and some toast, and began making calls to my mum and my friends to tell them all our good news.

The feeling of joy and happiness was overwhelming. Yet again, I had managed to bring a beautiful baby into this world despite being so fearful. And again, I felt so empowered, so happy and pleased that my revenge plan was going as well as I could hope.

Anna came home from her grandma's, jumped onto the bed next to me and I handed her sister to her. It was a beautiful moment.

CHAPTER TWENTY-ONE

RUNNING

I decided to start running after I had Mimi to try and lose some of the weight I had put on during my pregnancy, but I had never really tried running before. I think it appealed to me because I could just put my shoes on and leave the house. No gym to drive to, no personal trainer to meet, no class to attend – just the road and me. Perfect!

It was challenging at first: I had to do a combination of walking and running to build my endurance, and I had to learn how to breathe properly. During this process, I discovered that I'd been a shallow breather all my life and, believe me, it's really hard to take shallow breaths and run at the same time! After a while, I became more comfortable with breathing that was not only deeper, but also in rhythm with my strides. Every time I went out, I would use the lamp posts as markers, nudging myself to go a little bit further without stopping to walk and catch my breath.

As my strength developed, the walking segments became shorter and the running segments grew longer until eventually I could do an entire run without walking. I knew things were progressing when I started to look forward to running. Better still, I found I could go out and just lose myself with no interruptions. I had no keys, no money, no phone – and I felt anonymous. And as a family, we all loved fitness, so I received encouragement from them all.

I was losing weight and getting fitter but, more importantly, I felt free when I was running. My runs started to get longer too: twenty minutes turned into half an hour, which turned into forty-five minutes. To determine the right distance of a run, I would drive a route in my car and measure the miles, taking the guesswork out of the equation. All said and done, with some stretching included, I was usually out of the house for an hour at a time.

Once I had got over the initial learning curve of becoming a runner, I developed a good running speed and style. It evolved into a personal retreat for me, a place to do a lot of thinking – or *no* thinking – and I felt refreshed afterwards. I discovered the 'runners' high' I'd heard about, the released endorphins I didn't know I had.

It kind of turned into a religion for me, like a moving meditation, and it helped to calm my busy mind. I found that I could switch from the busyness of everything to simply focusing on my steps, my breath and my surroundings. That said, I still battled internally with my fears and still had concerns about my safety, so I only went running in the daytime and mainly on the streets to avoid any secluded areas. Sometimes I got comments from guys and beeps from men in cars, but I just ignored them or, if I was feeling brave, gave them the finger! I noticed that I no longer crossed a street to avoid a man coming the other way on the pavement. Sure, doing that would make a run much harder! But I just didn't feel the need anymore.

After a few months, as my body grew fitter and stronger, I also felt emotionally healthier. Both my body and mind were in the best shape they had been for a long while. Once I'd started to run a few times a week on a regular basis, I loved it.

Someone suggested to me that I should run in the Glasgow Women's 10k road race, which took place every year and attracted thousands of women. I signed up to, trained for and completed it with a sea of other women. It started at the Kelvingrove Art Gallery and Museum and weaved through the streets of the West End, finishing at Great Western Road. There were bagpipers playing at every kilometre to mark the distance and loads of bands along the way to motivate and serenade us. A Glasgow women's drumming band sent us off and we finished to the unmistakable sound of a steel band.

The atmosphere was amazing and there was such a buzz to it – I was hooked. So many women of all shapes, sizes and abilities took part, and the camaraderie was so inviting. Not only did I finish my first race without stopping, I was happy with my time. Running gave me an opportunity to set goals and achieve them while getting stronger and healthier along the way.

It was about this time that I was introduced to a woman named Shelley, who, like me, was a Londoner living in Glasgow, was married to a Glaswegian, and loved running. We clicked straight away; it felt like I had always known her and we started to go running together at least once a week.

It was great having a running partner – it meant I could take routes that I wouldn't have dared take alone. She knew of a great route in a park near our homes, which was mostly off the main path. It was nice and quiet and we didn't see many people. There was something so peaceful and healing about running through the woods, and I really looked forward to it. I felt so much more connected to the planet and myself when I was running in nature.

Not only did our running develop, but our relationship did too. We used the time to catch up with each other and chat; I was now able to run and speak at the same time without being out of breath! We laughed a lot because she was very competitive and would run slightly ahead of me, always wanting to beat me. But once I pointed that out, she would throttle back and run with me.

Our chats developed into more than just catching up and I found myself telling her about my past and what was done to me. It was really the first time I had opened up to someone in

Glasgow in such a personal way. I'm not sure why I did, but I felt safe with her and got a sense that she really understood what I was telling her. It felt good to share it with her. We both shared a lot on our runs and they became very therapeutic.

But we did more than just talk: we were always looking to improve our speed for races, something we were doing many more of. I also joined a running group at my gym to push myself even more. Determined to get my 10k time under 50 minutes, I thought they'd help make that a reality. My only hesitation about training with the group was that they ran at night, but I figured I'd be OK running in the dark among the safety of many people, including men. Or so I thought.

We all started off together, but then the faster ones pulled farther away until I was left with one guy at the back, which was fine – until he twisted his ankle and had to stop. I carried on, but quickly became aware of how my fear was creeping in more and more with every stride. Now I found myself constantly looking over my shoulder, and by the end of the run I was a worn-out, nervous wreck.

I was so annoyed at myself. Although I had genuinely worked out a lot of my fears, especially through running, this just showed me how deeply rooted and embedded inside me they still were. However, it didn't stop me from running – I just stuck to daytime runs with Shelley and never went back to the group. I think it would be fair to say we were both fairly obsessed with running. When my last child, Leila, was born in August 2001 (another wonderful home birth), I even bought a special runner's buggy so I could keep on training and eliminate the need for a babysitter.

Over the years, Shelley and I completed many 5k, 10k and half marathons in and around Glasgow, but we decided that we needed to take the ultimate challenge, and signed up to do the Edinburgh Marathon in June 2003. We stepped up our training, both on the road and in the gym, and followed a marathon programme spanning three months, slowly adding more distance to our runs during the week and to our already long Sunday runs. Before we knew it, we were out for three hours at a time on Sundays, covering ever more miles. We planned our routes, stashed water bottles in people's hedges to pick up along the way, and knew the locations of all the toilets. Out in all weather, nothing put us off. I have memories of running in snow when most people had a hard time just walking on the pavements.

People we knew noticed us out on our runs, and very often the first thing they would ask me about when I saw them was, 'How's the running going?' I felt like a real runner.

Shelley and I did our final, long training run, 21 miles, just a few weeks before the big race. It felt great and made me realise that our goal of completing the marathon was not only achievable, but that it might not be a huge, pain-riddled struggle for either of us. I was cautiously optimistic. But just a few days after that, Shelley told me she couldn't go through with it because she had discovered she was expecting her fourth child. I was happy for her on the one hand and devastated for both of us on the other. We'd trained so hard – what should I do? I was so ready and able to do this, but could I do it without her? Would I feel safe travelling by myself to Edinburgh overnight and running without her by my side?

I decided that I had to go, that I couldn't waste all my training. Shelley encouraged me, too. Luckily for me, when I got to the hotel in Edinburgh, I met someone I knew and he and his wife took me under their wing. Then I came across a couple of women I knew from Glasgow who were also in the race and staying in the hotel. Together we all went to a pasta party the night before, which was good fun and put me completely at ease.

I had arranged to run with someone I knew from my gym, and we started together, but it soon became clear that I was much faster and he was slowing me down: my goal was to get a time of under four hours and I couldn't do it by running with him. He could tell that he was slowing me down and encouraged me to take off without him – so I did.

It was during the marathon that I did something I wouldn't have normally done, but had been recommended to do at the pasta party as a distraction: I started to speak to people. I ran with a nurse for a while who was great, but she got tired and had to stop. The field of runners became especially thin and spread out during a stretch through a park, and I found myself running at the same pace as a man. I was already apprehensive about speaking to strangers, let alone strange men, but engaging with this man would be a particular challenge.

Covered head to toe in tattoos, he was exactly the kind of guy I would ordinarily have stayed far away from. I would have imagined the worst. Yet there we were, running really well together, so I decided to be brave and start a chat with him. He told me all about his tattoos and what they meant to him. It was something I had never thought about before; I'd just assumed it was body art and I'd never realised the significance and depth that could lie behind the ink. He helped open my eyes to something I had never even thought to look at before.

But he also needed to stop! So I completed my race alongside another man who was older, had children the same age as mine and was from North London too. He was lovely and helped make the last few miles, very tough ones indeed, that much easier. I was delighted when I crossed the finish line in 3 hours 57 minutes, not just for my time, but so many other reasons too.

I had faced down many fears by going through with the race even though I'd wanted to cancel when Shelley withdrew. I travelled by myself, stayed overnight in a hotel room alone and spoke to and connected with men I'd never met along the route. It was a lot, facing all of those fears over one weekend; it showed me that doing certain things may frighten me, but that doesn't have to stop me.

I carried on running for years after that, until I decided I hated the competitiveness at the races as well as the disappointment of being two seconds slower than my last race, so I stopped all races and just ran for myself. However, something started to dawn on me: while I was telling myself I felt free and grounded by my running, I realised I wasn't grounded at all. In fact, I started to understand that I was running both physically and emotionally, and that it wasn't helping me to be or stay grounded at all. So one day, I hung up the running shoes and there they stayed.

CHAPTER TWENTY-TWO

COLLEGE

I had been working as a volunteer at Women's Aid for about two years when the organisation secured sufficient funding to create a new, paid position for me. I became a follow-on worker, which meant that I supported women who had left our refuge and been rehoused out in the community, offering both practical and emotional support. I also ran a weekly support group consisting of the women living in the community as well as those still in the refuge.

I loved working with women and was still amazed and humbled every day by their strength, watching them arrive with nothing, move into the refuge and then start over again in a new home, out in the town. In most cases, I discovered, they held it together emotionally while they lived in the refuge, but then released a large proportion of the pent-up emotions once they were outside the refuge, in their own homes. It was as if they were finally, truly safe to acknowledge what they had been through. They needed the time and the right space to completely let go and open up.

I was able to listen to them, but felt I could be giving them so much more if I were therapeutically trained, so in 2004 I decided to do a counselling course. I researched a lot of courses, but couldn't decide which model best suited me. I liked some bits of many programmes, but not one entire modality – they all felt too restrictive. Then I came across a college which offered an integrative model, taking the best from three different approaches of counselling (person-centred therapy or PCT, rational emotive behaviour therapy or REBT, and gestalt) and putting them all together in one course. It looked as though it worked with clients in a very human and present way, incorporating both mind and body.

Ron and Jane, a married couple, owned and ran the college. I called and arranged a meeting with Jane, who was warm, personable and quickly made me feel at ease. The college was set in their family home and didn't feel like a college at all, which also appealed to me. She explained that the programme would take place over ten weekends a year for three years; we would get placements with clients, we were expected to write essays and we would hand in tape recordings of our sessions with clients to be analysed and evaluated.

It all sounded so good to me that I found myself signing up right there and then. But when I looked at the dates of the ten weekends, I realised that I couldn't make most of them. So Jane decided, given that I had been a support worker for about ten years and was still a volunteer at Rape Crisis, it would be OK for me to start as a second-year student. Not only would I finish school in two years rather than three, the weekends scheduled for the second-year students worked much better for me. I was excited to get started.

There were fifteen students in my section and we all had different backgrounds and experiences. The work was very experiential and it was like nothing I had ever done before. I found myself feeling a bit shy and insecure around people, which surprised me. We worked on each other for practice, and when we role-played as a client, we could either bring up a real personal issue of our own or one from the clients we'd been working with. I found both to be hugely beneficial.

A lot of the coursework was based on our personal development, so in addition to practising our counselling skills on others, we worked on establishing a better connection to ourselves, which was ultimately what we wanted for our clients. This involved mirror work, empty chair work, music therapy, breath work and, twice a year, residential weekends where we all stayed on campus for three days and three nights of intensive training.

We often worked in a way that I called 'the goldfish bowl' – and for obvious reasons. It consisted of two students, sitting face to face in the middle of the room, with one student playing the role of client and the other the role of therapist. The rest of us would sit in a circle around them and watch their session. It terrified me. I was scared that I would be too vulnerable as a client or they would see I didn't know what I was doing as a therapist. I much preferred working in smaller groups or pairs; they weren't so overwhelming for me. The goldfish bowl is a very direct approach to counselling and can feel extremely challenging from the client's point of view, but it was also a lot of pressure for the therapists. Our tutors would stop the sessions constantly with their feedback and I watched many students get flustered, myself included.

One of the residential weekend training sessions was based on a 'Gestalt' exercise. Our class spent the whole weekend (eating, sleeping and working) in the basement rooms of the college. They kept our watches and removed the clocks. We weren't allowed to speak, except for work, even during our break time. We couldn't drink tea or coffee and there was no smoking allowed; we ate only porridge and fruit. It stretched all of us.

Working in pairs, we sat opposite each other while maintaining solid eye contact with our partner, taking turns asking and answering questions. For example, one of us would ask the question, 'Can you tell me who you are?' When the other thought they had the answer, they would go and find one of the tutors and tell them. If they were 'right', the tutor would then give us another question to work on. It seemed innocuous enough. Many times, I thought I had the answer ('I'm a mother, wife, woman, daughter, sister...') and would go along and tell one of the tutors, but I kept getting sent back without a new question. My answers weren't 'right'.

At some point, while my partner asked me that same question again, I had a very unexpected reaction, one that I did not see coming. Images of that night when I was thirteen shot across the screen in my mind – vivid images I'd not remembered before. I saw myself lying on the floor of the bedroom, tied up by my right wrist and right ankle to the pipes of a radiator. I saw Randall holding the knife against my throat to silence me. I also saw him stabbing me, plunging the knife into my vagina. Another scene appeared: I watched the two boys leave the room, and then Randall came back alone and urinated all over me, laughing because I had already peed myself. As I recognised those dirty, shameful feelings that I'd felt for years rising up inside of me, I instantly felt sick deep in the pit of my stomach. I tried to put the images out of my mind, but I couldn't – they were too strong, too clear, too real.

I was so confused. I didn't remember getting stabbed that night or being peed on. Where were these memories coming from? How did I not remember them before? And worse than that, what did this say about me as a person? Was this who I was? Was I always going to be defined as the woman who had been raped or was there more to me? I really thought I had dealt with my past because I had managed to get over the biggest hurdle I thought I faced, which was having children. What else was locked in my mind? What else would I have to get over?

I remained sitting opposite my partner, struggling to hold it together, but the tears started to fall from my eyes, slowly at first, and then uncontrollably. My body began to shake and shake, and I couldn't stop it. So many thoughts and images were coming up, all at the same time.

I got up and went to find one of my tutors, composing myself on the way, and told her I had the answer to the question. She asked the question one more time: 'Can you tell me who you are?' This time I replied, 'I'm me!' and started to cry all over again. It was so powerful. I realised right then that it wasn't the answer we gave them that was important, but the journey we took to achieve it.

Over the duration of the weekend, my body responded many more times with uncontrollable shaking. Every now and again, one of the tutors would come by and tell me to open my mouth and breathe. I was obviously holding on, both physically and emotionally. The training came to an end on the Sunday night and we were led upstairs to a feast of food, which, after our Spartan diet, was a welcome and lovely change. Everyone was feeling very relieved and happy it was over, but for me, it felt like the start of something – and it was.

That weekend showed me many things. Clearly, I was in denial about my past. Yes, I had done enough work to have three children, but my past was still affecting me and I wasn't as healed as I wanted to think I was. I gave off the image that everything was OK, and wore a mask to promote that image, but at college they saw through that and with all the work we were doing, the cracks had begun to show. My mind had convinced me and everyone else that I was in control, but what did that mean, anyway? I wasn't very spontaneous in life, due to my need to have everything under control, and my need to feel safe kept me locked in. I could see that my life was restrictive and not very free at all. And I kept coming back to the same question: will I ever get past this or will it always haunt me? I also realised that if it was still affecting me, it was still holding back a large part of me, too; I wasn't being real. I felt like a fake, wearing a fake smile most of the time, and pretending everything was OK.

During the week, we met with our tutors for one-to-ones to see how we were doing after the residential weekend. I explained to Jane what was coming up for me, that I hadn't been able to put the images out of my mind and was having trouble sleeping because they were appearing in my dreams, too, waking me up. She said that if I decided to work on it and explore it further through therapy, her husband Ron would be the best person to do so with because he was very good with trauma. The next day, I called to make my first appointment.

That weekend was near the end of my counselling course and graduation was not far away, but the events from that weekend also made me decide to stay on for another year and complete the psychotherapy course, because clearly I had some personal work to do. I thought: how could I be a good therapist with such unfinished business? How could I expect my clients to go to difficult places in themselves if I couldn't do it for myself? I wanted to clean it up and it felt like I had no choice but to go back to therapy again and to do a year of coursework focusing on psychotherapy.

CHAPTER TWENTY-THREE

THERAPY

I didn't know Ron, Jane's husband, too well. During our residential weekends, he would come into classes and take over for a spell, or sit and observe and then give feedback. I knew he would be our teacher for the psychotherapy year. He had designed the course and clearly had an amazing mind, but I felt intimidated by him: he was very direct and challenging in his approach, which at times felt brutal, but also very honest.

His office was in the basement, apart from the classrooms and workspaces upstairs, and I felt insecure being away from the other people. As I approached his door, I felt my heart beating faster and faster. I had never asked for this kind of help from a man before. On top of that, he was American, just as the boys were. We sat down in the wooden chairs that faced each other and he asked me what I wanted to work on. I told him about the new memories I'd had over the residential weekend and that I wanted to focus our work on what had happened to me when I was thirteen so I could get some peace and resolution with it all.

My idea of 'working on it' was to find a way to get rid of it by pushing it back down so it wouldn't affect me anymore. Ron's approach was the exact opposite: to really learn to be OK with it all, I would need to face it, to finally accept what was done. He asked me if I was prepared to do that, no matter what I had to face. Even though I was so nervous inside and felt unsafe, and was worried that I could re-traumatise myself again by bringing it all into the light of day, I heard my voice saying yes.

According to our model of counselling, I had been assessed as a 'targeted client', which meant I was ready to work. It didn't feel like it though – I had a lot of fears bubbling up all the time. A big wave of fear came up as I sat talking to my new therapist, the man who owned and ran my school. What would he really think of me when he heard the details of that night? Would he be disgusted? Would it change what he thought about me? That fear, those thoughts showed me that so much of my self-identity was still defined by the rape if I continued to carry those old assumptions around with me.

The first few sessions were spent mainly discussing my thoughts on what it would look and feel like if I were to go back into it all. I told Ron I was scared that the internal darkness I'd lived with for years when I was younger would come back and that I would be overwhelmed by it all and get caught up in it again. It felt so risky, but I also realised that I had been pretending to myself for all these years that I had completely dealt with it, and I'd had enough of the ripple effects it created in my life. I'd told myself I was free of it all, despite feelings and actions to the contrary. I told Ron I was so nervous, but that I felt that I had no choice but to work on it in order to stop dragging my past into my future.

After the first few sessions he said to me it would be a good idea if I could tell him what they did to me since I hadn't mentioned any details yet. I felt sick with shame and guilt, but knew I had to try and find the courage to share – not for him, but for me. Yet it was so hard to find my voice, and I felt as though I had instantly regressed back into that thirteen-year-old girl who was too scared to speak.

I had seen many counsellors in the past when I was trying to get pregnant, and could see the shock in their eyes when I told them just a few of the details of what was done to me. As soon as I saw that, I knew I couldn't work with them – it would be too much for them to hear. When I looked into Ron's eyes, I got the sense that he could take what I was going to say.

He picked up on my fear so we established some ground rules; in particular, I could stop if it got too much. Once we agreed to that, I began to tell the story of that night. I went into great detail about buying the alcohol and being in the café. At this point he stopped me and told me to just start from when they put me in the bedroom: in other words, to stop delaying and get to the point.

I started to tell him how they had undressed me and put me on the floor and held the knife to my throat to shut me up. Then I saw the image of Randall kicking me between my legs with his boots on. Instantly, I felt the pain again in my body, which shocked me – and then the shaking that I had experienced during the residential weekend started again in my legs. I couldn't control them. Ron told me not to worry about the shaking, that it was normal, and that trauma gets trapped in the cells in our body and the shaking was simply the trauma and fear being released.

I looked into his eyes and could see he was OK, that he wasn't disgusted and was staying steady with all that he was hearing. It reassured me that I could work with him even though the process was really uncomfortable for me.

I had such mixed feelings towards my therapy sessions; I hated going, but something inside of me was driving me to go. There was a knowing inside that I needed to do this. It was as if that residential weekend had opened the vault door that I had kept locked and sealed for so many years; I had to keep going.

With each session, more and more of the story came out of my mouth and I was surprised by how much there was to tell. The sessions would leave me exhausted and emotionally drained because I couldn't make sense of it all. Where were these memories coming from? Could I trust them? Had

I made them up? After all, I had heard so many women's stories in the course of my work – maybe I had just got mine confused with theirs?

I would voice these fears to Ron and he would answer with, 'Well, why would you make it up? And if you did want to make something up about yourself, wouldn't you choose something better?' That did make me think.

Over the span of these sessions my dreams started to change, and still more and more information was revealed to me during my nights. The nightmares would wake me up, and often the first thing I saw when I woke up was their faces hovering over me. I would thrash about in bed and scream out, telling them to stop and leave me alone, then wake in a panic. Soon I began to dread going to sleep and tried to delay it, thinking that if I didn't sleep, then I wouldn't have nightmares. As a mum of three girls this wasn't very practical; I was worn out most of the time. I also felt bad for what it must have been doing to Steven, trying to sleep next to me while all the thrashing and screaming was going on.

Alongside having therapy, I was still on the course studying psychotherapy, which also challenged my personal development. One weekend our whole group watched a 'goldfish bowl' session between two students. One of the students was role-playing a client of his, a woman who had been stabbed, and he was very good at it. As he was speaking, I began to feel the shaking building up inside my body. The more the session carried on, the worse I felt. My legs started shaking; I put my hands on them to try and keep them still, but they wouldn't stop. I felt panicky and dizzy and sick, and worried that other people would notice. Rather than stop my legs from shaking, my hands joined in with them and shook as well. I felt tears pricking my eyes, and the sick feeling kept building to the point where I ran out of the class as fast as I could and threw up in the toilet.

I was so embarrassed that my classmates had seen me like this that rather than go back to the group, I went into the kitchen to hide and settle down for a while. But after a short time, a woman sent to find me approached quietly, said I was shaking and held my hand. She said they were waiting for me so together we went back in. I couldn't look at anyone; I felt the old feelings of contamination all over me and thought they would be disgusted. My shame felt like an old, heavy, familiar cloak covering me.

Ron, who was instructing the class, was very supportive and explained to everyone that I had chosen to work through a violent and traumatic event and that I was brave for facing it. He must have sensed my feelings of shame, and he encouraged me to look at everyone individually to see what their eyes said back to me. Slowly, I raised my head and one by one I made eye contact with everyone in the group. Some were smiling, others held my gaze, some had tears – but there was no disgust from any of them. It was hard to hold their gazes but it helped me to see that what I told myself (that people would be disgusted if they knew the truth about me) wasn't true. It was a good reference for my mind; I was learning to stay with the evidence I could see and not my assumptions in my head.

As the course went on, more and more about that night would surface, always catching me off guard. We spent a good bit of time doing breath work, which was really just sitting on the floor, listening to music and simply being with our breath. I discovered it was much more powerful than I thought it would be.

Ron was trained not only in psychotherapy, but also in therapeutic bodywork, which helps to release trapped emotions in the body. It was very normal for him to come around the class and do some bodywork on people while we were doing breath work, but he generally left me alone because he knew I still struggled to be touched by men. He once tried to touch me, but I pushed him away. Usually, he just encouraged me to loosen my jaw and let some breath out.

One day I was sitting against the wall breathing and watching him work with a woman in my class. He was massaging her neck and then straddled her to get into a better position. It was nothing unusual for a massage therapist to do, and I understood that very well, but the next thing I knew I was backing into the corner of the room and I could hear someone screaming and screaming. It was me. Again I was so embarrassed and confused. All these body memories were spilling out of me and it felt like I had no control over them. I also wondered why, if these memories were so clear, did I not remember them before? Yes, I obviously understood the effects of trauma and PTSD – the mind can shut out traumatic memories for years until a person is ready to face them. But somehow, even after all these years of working with Women's Aid and the Rape Crisis centre, and hearing countless stories of rape and assault that I could relate to so well, I still felt that it didn't apply to me.

Ron came to me later and asked if I was OK. 'Where did that come from?' I asked him in turn. He laughed and said it came from me. That afternoon, while doing more breath work, he came over and sat down facing me, and asked if it would be all right to hold my hands. He encouraged me to make eye contact with him and very quickly I felt all my shame build up again. Once again the tears flowed and I started to cry and cry. I wanted to look away but he suggested that staying with it would be a good way for me to break the shame. So I looked into his eyes, again saw no disgust coming from him, and carried on with the exercise. It absolutely helped to dissipate some of the shame, but I still had a long way to go.

Over the three years that I had personal therapy, more and more memories emerged – all of which I had never remembered before. Most of them came at night in my dreams, and although the things I saw were disturbing and challenging, it was an easier way for me to process what had happened. It was the memories, the flashbacks that came during the day, triggered by simple and everyday things, which were the hardest to take.

Wherever I was and whatever I was doing, the flashbacks

would paralyse me for that moment and I'd be caught up, both emotionally and physically, in what my mind was showing me. In one such flashback I was forced to perform oral sex on one of the boys and then vomited after he ejaculated in my mouth. A rush of nausea hit me deep in my gut and I felt like I was going to throw up – and I did. It showed me that while I didn't completely trust my mind and was still confused by the memories, I knew I couldn't force my body to react the way it was doing: I had to trust my body.

There were so many triggers for flashbacks that navigating a day without them was seemingly impossible. The list included: men with long hair; baseball or heavy metal jackets; men who smelt of cigarettes or alcohol; body odour; walking past two or more men, something I thought I'd got over; the sound of an American accent coming from a man, another thing I thought I'd worked through; being around men who were drinking; reading or hearing a story about rape; and the layout of rooms where the doors and radiators were positioned similarly to those in the room in London.

By now I was having flashbacks of so many different scenarios from that night, it was beginning to feel like there was a constant porn movie running through my head – and that was tough. I had read a lot about false memories, and I wondered if that was what was going on with me. But then I would think of my body and how it reacted, and I couldn't find an explanation for that. I would tell myself that if these memories were made up, I would stop my body from reacting the next time it happened. Then I tried, but I couldn't do it. Once my mind and body connected with a memory, the tears, trembling, nausea and physical pains would follow. Not only that, but I would experience the same contorted patterns in my body: my hands would turn into fists, my legs would thrash about and try to get away, my right arm and right leg would struggle to be free, and I would rub my arms and legs in disgust as if I were trying to rub the smell of the boys off myself.

After all that work and therapy, one thing became clear: it wasn't so much the memories of what they did to me that disturbed me, but rather my strong resistance towards accepting it. I found that fighting with the memories was worse and was creating a battle inside me, leaving me constantly unsettled, uneasy and unable to completely process what had happened.

CHAPTER TWENTY-FOUR

MUM'S SECRET

After about a year of therapy, I told my mum that I had gone back to it again, for what had happened to me when I was younger. Whenever we talked, she would ask how it was going; I would just say, 'Oh, fine,' without giving any real details. Once, during a visit to her home in London, everyone else had gone to bed and I was sitting alone with Mum in the lounge when she asked me again how the therapy was going. This time I told her some details and I got quite emotional in the process. She comforted me while I cried.

And then she told me something that caught me completely by surprise. She said that when she was eight years old she too had been raped several times, by a neighbour. Her mum used to encourage her to go round and play with his daughter (who was her friend), and somehow she knew he would take advantage of her if she did. She tried to tell her mum that she didn't want to go over, but she'd get told off for being rude.

Eventually, she told her brother, Anthony, who then went on to tell my grandparents. The man was charged and it went to court. Not only was he found guilty, but they also discovered he had been raping his daughters, too. While he was in prison, my mum and her family moved away and they never spoke of it again.

Mum told me that for years she'd thought it was her fault she'd been raped, but in time and with age, she realised it wasn't. She explained that after he'd been arrested, she had to be examined by the police, looking for evidence; she said it was almost as bad as being raped. When I'd told her, years before, what had happened to me and that I didn't want to go to the police, she didn't encourage me to do so because she didn't want me to go through that as well.

All those years of thinking she hadn't believed me instantly melted away with this new knowledge, and I suddenly understood why she'd behaved as she had. It made perfect sense. I had held a grudge against her for more than twenty years without having any clue of what she herself had gone through. And despite having five children with him, and being married for thirty-eight years, she never told my dad. He died without knowing this about his wife. She told me that if she had said why she didn't want me to go to the police, then she would have had to tell her story too – and that she could not do.

I felt so sad for my mum, that she had kept this completely to herself all those years without ever having received any support. Though amazed by her resilience, I was heartbroken at the same time. I wondered just how many women must be in her position, too.

She felt guilty that she hadn't protected me when I was younger and thought it was all her fault that it had happened to me. We held each other's hands and cried.

I had no idea she felt this way and I had to reassure her that it wasn't her fault, the same way it wasn't my grandparents' fault that it happened to her. The sharing did something to our relationship; it brought about a new closeness, which I was (and still am) so grateful for. It also helped me to understand her reaction after she'd read the note I'd left on my pillow so many years before – and why I was confused by it. Within minutes, the resentment I'd harboured towards my mother for so long completely melted away.

CHAPTER TWENTY-FIVE

EMAHÓ

During my first year at college, I heard a lot of students talk very enthusiastically about a workshop they had attended given by a man called Emahó. My tutor, Ron, had been going to him for many years, too. I knew virtually nothing about him or the work he did, but curiosity got the better of me and I decided to attend one of his workshops and find out for myself.

I had a look at his website and learned that he was a Native American, living in Santa Fe, that he referred to himself as a 'teacher of life' and that he'd been doing seminars since 1990. From the schedule I could see that he toured Europe twice a year, once in the spring and once in the autumn, going to pretty much the same cities each time. Glasgow was a regular stop for him. It didn't really say much more than that.

In the autumn of 2005, I went along with a few friends from college to his seminar, held in a big, old converted church in the Gorbals section of town. By the time we arrived, there were already about 200 people creating quite a sound in the cavernous space. I heard lots of different European accents as people were hugging and kissing, saying hello. They all seemed to know each other. It made me feel terribly uncomfortable – they were very openly affectionate with each other and I wasn't used to that. Also, given the new setting, I felt incredibly shy and awkward among these strangers. One thing was familiar: a lot of the music I heard that day I recognised from our weekends at college.

My friends told me that Emahó was a shaman but I didn't really know what that meant. They said that he would first give a talk, then set up his *mesa* (which means 'table' in Spanish, but 'altar' in this context) and end with a fire dance. We found seats near the front – they said it was better to be nearer although I didn't understand that either. Then we waited for him to start.

A small man – well-dressed in a white shirt, black suit and tie, with dark skin and long, silver hair pulled back neatly into a ponytail – walked up to the front of the room. I was mesmerised by him, but not because of how he looked or how he dressed: there was so much light surrounding him, more than I'd ever seen around anyone else. For as long as I can remember, I've been able to see and feel people's vibrations; it's how I sense them. With Emahó, I could see an uninterrupted brightness all around the outline of him. To me, he just glowed, inside and out. I've also seen the opposite: with Randall, I saw uninterrupted blackness, and given what I felt from inside him, I knew he was dangerous.

Before Emahó spoke, he looked everybody in the eye, connecting with and acknowledging each and every one of us. He took his time doing so, and with so many of us, it took a while. When he looked at me, and it was only for a few moments, it felt as if he could see inside me, *really* see who I was. It was paradoxically unnerving and comforting at the same time. He then began to speak; his voice was warm and he used clear, simple words. He stood in place as he spoke, moving his head to look around the room at us, but otherwise remained motionless. Everything he said felt personal, as if he were aiming his speech directly at me.

The teaching he gave that day was about what can happen to us as children, saying that if nothing traumatic happens to us by the time we are thirteen then we will most likely be fine going into adulthood. That was the exact age that I'd been raped. It made me wonder how different my life might have been if this hadn't happened to me – and right at the cut-off age. What would my life look like now? I felt profound sadness for what my thirteen-year-old self had to go through, but I also felt intense anger towards the two young men whose cruel actions were still affecting my life.

At times, I found it very difficult to keep my eyes open while he spoke. It was as if I had jet lag despite the fact that I'd only driven across town. I wondered if my mind was shutting down, unable to process all of what he was saying; I also suspected I was affected by the light radiating out of him.

After his talk, people queued at the back of the room to speak with him and ask him questions. I so wanted to speak to him as well, but I felt too shy and stayed away.

After talking with everyone in the queue, he went over to a table along the back wall and took from it a black cloth with a red border around the edges. He then walked to the centre of the room, laid the cloth out on the floor and sat, cross-legged, in front of it. Clearly, people already knew he would do this: several were already sitting on the floor, forming an incomplete circle with Emahó in the middle. I asked one of my friends what was happening. She told me that he was setting up the *mesa* for the ceremony, or fire dance, to follow. What on earth is a fire dance? I wondered.

A woman brought over a stack of leather pouches and put them down on the floor next to Emahó. He opened the pouches one by one, removed their contents and placed each item very carefully on the black cloth. I didn't understand why he was placing certain objects where he did, but clearly there was intent behind the location of each of them. More people sat on the floor, filling in the spaces, until there was a full circle around him. Others then stood behind those sitting in order to get a better view. Everyone, whether sitting or standing, remained very still, closely watching his every move. Again, I was mesmerised. I didn't really understand what each object was or what they represented, but I was drawn in: it wasn't what he placed down on the cloth that touched me, but rather the way in which he did it, with so much reverence and respect for each item. It was one of the most beautiful things I had ever seen and it moved me to tears.

He was deliberate with his motions, so focused and present throughout the process. There was music playing while he worked and it added another dimension to what he was doing, another layer of beauty. In sharp contrast to when I'd entered the room a couple of hours before, you could have heard a pin drop between each song. More items were brought to him, including two tall candles in brass candle holders (designed to look like fish) and a pair of eagle wings, joined together to form a 'V' shape.

After he'd placed the candles and all the objects from the many pouches in very specific places on the *mesa*, the same woman brought over a yellowish piece of cloth and a large bouquet of roses. He covered one of his legs with the cloth and then laid the roses on top of it, protecting himself from the thorns. With a knife, he then sliced about half of each stem away, scraped the thorns from the remaining stems, then very delicately placed each prepared rose on the *mesa*, adding colour and still more beauty.

His final act of preparation was to light the two tall candles that stood on the *mesa*. Again, he did so with slow, deliberate movement, using the same matchstick to light both. He moved so slowly that I thought the matchstick would burn out before he lit the second candle, but a tiny flicker of flame allowed him to finish the preparation. He stood and then very slowly backed away, keeping his eyes on the *mesa* the whole time. When he'd gone about ten feet, he turned and walked to the back of the room.

People broke away, moving to the corners of the room and areas against the walls, to change their clothes for the ceremony – and they did so right there in the main hall! I felt embarrassed as they all very naturally stripped down – I didn't know where to look. The men changed mostly into shorts and T-shirts while the women mostly wore summer dresses or long skirts and T-shirts. I sought the privacy of the bathroom to change my clothes.

People milled about while Emahó was off getting changed; some were eating or drinking by the refreshment table, some were quietly chatting and others remained seated in the circle on the floor, staying quiet. I sat on a chair near a wall, watching all of it, not knowing what to make of any of it. The music, which continued to play, changed to the sound of llamas chanting. This seemed to prompt more people to sit around the circle, much as they had while Emahó prepared the *mesa*.

Emahó emerged from another room and looked completely transformed; he'd left the room looking like a man from the city and returned looking like a man from the jungle. He now wore a black apron with a red border, tied at the waist and covering his legs to just above the knees. Over the apron was an outer skirt with small bones carved into Buddhist figures, connected by tiny bones, beaded together, forming a crisscross pattern. On his upper body he wore a Native American battle breastplate, made up primarily of eagle bones that looked like small tubes laced together in rows. Around his upper arms and ankles were leather cuffs with Native American style hand-beaded flying eagles, edged with tiny bells. He wore carved bone guards on his forearms. Tied just above his knees were straps with bells, designed for dances. His hair, pulled neatly into a ponytail while he'd spoken, was down – and it gave him a wilder look. I felt a bit uneasy; I didn't know what to expect, and even though it hadn't really begun, I'd already never seen anything like it – or him – before. I really didn't know what I thought.

Emahó walked around and around, inside the circle of sitting people, sometimes stopping to change direction. He did that for several minutes until the chanting stopped, replaced by what sounded like tribal drums playing a repetitive, ten-beat rhythm. As soon as the drums started, everybody got up and formed four quadrants, like squares opposite each other, leaving a square-shaped empty space in between the quadrants, with the *mesa* in the middle of the empty space. Everyone stood facing the direction of the *mesa*. Then we all started dancing, as if walking or jogging in place, each step in unison with the ten beats of the drums. On Emahó's cue, the opposing quadrants of people moved towards each other, filling the empty space between the quadrants, and stopped moving forward when they reached the *mesa*. They stayed dancing in that location for about a minute and then, again on Emahó's cue, moved back to their original locations. First, one set of opposing quadrants would move towards and away from each other, and then the other quadrants would do the same thing. My friends explained that this was a 'warm-up'.

Then the drums stopped and a different kind of chanting came on. I later found out that it was a recording of Zulu warriors, acknowledging the bravery of their opponents before an imminent battle was to begin. It was a beautiful and chilling sound.

When the Zulus finished their battle cry, the warm-up was over. The lights dimmed, Emahó called out 'Drums!' and a new, steady track of drumming came over the speakers. The drums were loud and they spoke to my bones. We all broke out of the quadrants and again created a circle, seven or eight people deep, doing a kind of two-step dance to the beat, with Emahó and the *mesa* in the middle. I could feel my legs instinctively wanting to move with the drums and my feet were itching to dance straight away, but he'd said before the dance that it would be good for new people (like me) to first sit and watch for a while before dancing. So within a few moments, after Emahó took the first person to his *mesa*, I sat on the floor, very close to the *mesa*, so that I could get a clear and unobstructed view; I really wanted to see what he was going to do.

As everyone danced in place, doing a fast two-step and

rhythmic breathing with the beat, he would look into the crowd and find a person to bring back to the *mesa*. Once there, the person would kneel down as Emahó continued to dance next to them. I sat about three feet from the candles on the *mesa* – and these were not ordinary candles, they were about two feet long and had seven wicks in them. Each flame coming from these candles was big, roughly six to ten inches high. From my bird's-eye view, I watched him place his hands in the flames of the candles – and he'd keep them there for five, ten, twenty seconds in the considerable flames without any sign of pain or discomfort. His hands and his face were completely relaxed; he looked focused but steady, like a man doing a job that requires undivided attention. He would then touch the person with his hands, usually on their forehead or throat. It looked as if he were baptising them with fire. Some of it looked quite rough to me and I felt anxious, but I looked around and saw that no one seemed scared. Many were dancing, some were sitting and all were watching him.

I watched the people that he brought to the *mesa* very closely. Once on their knees, they put their heads back, exposing their throats. It was a position of real vulnerability and surrender yet they all looked so relaxed and trusting. He did different things, unique to each person, but he put his hands in the fire for each of them.

There was so much movement in the dance and the drums were very loud, but it seemed quiet, almost peaceful, sitting there so close to the *mesa*. After watching about two dozen or so people come to the *mesa*, I heard another sound – and this one really made me want to jump up and dance. It was a didgeridoo, being played just a few feet behind me. My body couldn't resist any longer; it was as if the drums and didgeridoo spoke to my bones and pulled me to my feet to join the others, dancing and breathing and sweating.

At first, I danced at the back, feeling a bit shy around all these people who had done this so many times before. But it didn't take long for me to forget about them and get totally caught up with the dance: my feet fell into the two-step move with ease and it seemed as though nothing else mattered but the dance. I wouldn't say that I was a fantastic dancer, but it felt great. My body felt freer than it had for ages, as if I were dancing for my life.

After Emahó had brought someone to the *mesa*, they would then either dance at the back of the group or sit down. This created a flow of dancers, moving from the back to the front as the ceremony progressed. So even though I had started out dancing behind everyone, I soon found myself near the action. Then it was my turn: I felt his hand on my shoulder, guiding me, as we danced together to the *mesa*. I felt so self-conscious because now all the people sitting had their eyes on me. As I knelt down, I looked at the candles right there in front of me and then closed my eyes. But it was hard to relax and I felt concerned. Just as I was having that thought, he leaned down and whispered in my ear, telling me to relax my neck, that I was too stiff. So I took a deep breath and did my best to relax.

I opened my eyes and watched his right hand, there in the tall, full flame, for what seemed like a very long time.

Slowly, he brought his hand towards my forehead. His palm was completely blackened by the soot and smoke. The touch of his hot hand on my forehead was like nothing I'd ever felt before: how could human flesh get so hot without burning? The heat transfer from his hand sent a shot through my entire body, like a wave of electricity. But I had also seen something else as Emahó's hand was moving towards me that I did not expect to see: another scene from that night. It was Randall, sitting by my side while I lay on the floor, naked, tied to the radiator by my right wrist and right ankle. He was trying to set my hair on fire with a lighter.

I struggled with this new information and thought maybe my mind was confused because of the environment I was in, that I had made it up. Emahó finished working on me and I got back to my feet. In a daze, I found a chair and sat down to watch the rest of the dance. To say I felt confused would be a dramatic understatement: what had just happened?

And that was just the first day of a four-day workshop.

Despite the fact that I felt scared, unsure of all the people in the room and uncertain of what was going on, I found myself going back for the next three days. I couldn't work out why I went back, but I just felt like I had to; I felt compelled. To my mind, it defied logic. Somehow, everything he spoke about made sense, and when I didn't get caught by my mind with all of my assumptions, insecurities and conditioning, I loved the dance.

I relaxed more and it got easier each day. But one thing did not change: every time Emahó brought me to the *mesa* to work on me, I got the same image of Randall, flicking his lighter and bringing it towards my hair. I saw this four times over the four dances.

I noticed there were a lot of children there so I brought Leila, my youngest daughter, who was four years old at the time, with me on the Sunday. She loved the dance, didn't question any of it and wasn't fazed at all. Emahó had given her a rose during the dance and she held onto it with pride. The fact that children weren't scared by the dance said a lot to me.

I decided at the end of the workshop that I would go up to Emahó and thank him. I knew somehow his words had impacted me and were embedded deep inside; I felt more alive than I had done for years.

I joined the lengthy queue and soon I was at the front. As I put my hand out to thank him, he gently took my hand in both of his and looked me in the eye. In that moment he felt so familiar to me, as if I had always known him: it was like coming home. I told him that the teaching from Thursday night had really touched me and that if I had not had a certain experience when I was thirteen, things would have been very different for me. He looked at me with such kindness, I started to cry – I knew that he understood me without needing any words.

He then took me by the arm, led me to his *mesa* and gave me the candles that had been used that night for the dance. I thanked him again and said goodbye.

I went back to his workshop in Glasgow the following March and, again, his words hit me so powerfully. He talked about our personal relationship to life and the 'human predicament' that we all find ourselves caught in. It enabled me to have more understanding into the struggles all people go through in their lives. We are all born in a similar state, like blank canvases, but we become corrupted and conditioned by our upbringing and the many events that shape us. It all happens silently without us even knowing it. We all have struggles and we all, in essence, can't help but do what we do. Once a person realises that they can't help but do what they do, they in turn have more compassion for others who also cannot help it. It's not an excuse or absolution for people's actions, rather an explanation of the mechanism behind them.

He spoke of our connection to ourselves and our hearts, and asked the question: 'Do we hold onto our hurt and disappointment for reasons that most of us don't explore, or can we let it go in order to be more alive?' It got me thinking about my hurt and my disappointment – was that what was holding me back?

I also read his book, *The Winds of Your Heart*, and so much of it resonated with me. After hearing him speak and reading his words, I asked the question: 'When will I let go of everything that was done to me?' I could see that I was holding on tightly to my hurt and disappointment, as well as resentment and vengeful thoughts against the boys. When I listened to my thoughts, I heard complaining about what had happened; it was clearer than ever that I'd let the hurt shape my life. I still had so much fear and anxiety heavily influencing my day-to-day life, colouring everything I did, and holding me back from living a full, spontaneous, happy life. I was keeping myself trapped, cloistered.

I continued to go back to the workshops in Glasgow for another year until I decided I didn't want to wait for six months until he returned to town. The fire dances and time with Emahó were opening doors in me and I was feeling more grounded than I had in a long time. I started to ask him questions too, usually about memories; I wanted to know if I could trust the memories and pictures that flooded my head. How could I know if they were true?

In the autumn of 2008, a friend of mine, Fi, was travelling to one of the workshops in Bremen, Germany, and she suggested that I come along with her. Despite having travelled by myself to run the marathon, it was still a struggle for me, so I happily accepted her offer. Not only did the prospect of travel frighten me, I was scared to go to a country that I'd never been to, filled with people I'd never met.

It was so different going to a workshop away from home. I could stay in the space it opened up in me without any interruptions from my family; it felt a lot more intense.

Fi would leave the workshop immediately after the dance, but now that I knew more people there, I would stay on and chat for a spell, meeting Fi later back at the hostel. And those walks back to the hostel were not easy: I felt intimidated by men who were hanging around on the street, drinking and hanging out. I also had to walk past some sex shops with their own unsavoury characters also out on the street. Add to that the fact that it was dark outside, and my heart pounded like a little bird's. But I knew that I had to start breaking my old fear patterns, so I used those walks as a way to become accustomed to walking alone rather than relying on people to always escort me home. It was important to show myself that I could do it – and I did.

The time in Bremen stands out in my mind for another reason. Something happened at the end of those dances that had never happened to me in Glasgow. After every fire dance, the crew working for Emahó always played the same beautiful song by Enya, sung in Gaelic, *Na Laetha Geal M'óige*. I had always liked the song, but I'd never had any particular reaction to it. When the song played in Bremen, I felt something build up deep inside me and I started to cry and cry, uncontrollably. I was so embarrassed; my loud sobs, along with Enya, filled the otherwise quiet room. The crying would start when the song did, and stop when it ended. I couldn't understand the words, yet they spoke to me about the struggles in life. The emotions came from a place so deep inside me that I was shocked by it.

While I sobbed, I could see all new images and information from that night, returning to me as if a dam had burst inside me. I felt such sadness and grief for my younger self, but at the same time, I had so many questions running through my head.

Why do we do this to each other? What's the point of all

this violence? And why does it have to happen? The questions just made me cry more and more. Then it hit me that I wasn't just crying for me: it was as if I felt the pain of every woman who had ever been raped and was reaching out to them, too. It wasn't just 'me' anymore; it was 'us'.

CHAPTER TWENTY-SIX

THE MONK

When new memories came back to me, they would haunt my dreams at night and disturb my mind during the day for weeks at a time. I still wasn't sure if the memories were of real events – and I wondered if I would ever really know.

The images of Randall that came to me in the fire dance, of him trying to set fire to my hair, began to evolve and unfold with each successive dance. At first I only saw Randall, but then my memories expanded to include more and more of what was going on in the room. As this particular memory of Randall unfolded, I noticed there was a third male present: a Tibetan monk. With each memory, I saw him more and more clearly. I thought to myself, my God, I'm really going mad now. How can this be? Yet the more I fought with myself over the memories, the more vivid they would become, forcing me to look at them.

In the scenes that I saw, the monk sat very calmly next to me on the floor, crossed-legged on my right-hand side, in between the radiator I was tied to and me. He looked about twenty years old, had very dark, short hair and was wearing a burgundy robe with an orange shawl over it. His robe had no collar or sleeves and there were thin blue borders around the hems at his upper arms. There were two orange triangles on the front of the robe and an orange square on the back.

Kneeling on the other side of my body, I saw Randall take a silver Zippo lighter from his pocket and then grab a load of my hair. He was laughing, saying, 'Let's burn the bitch, set her on fire!' He flicked it open and tried to light it over and over again. A flame would appear, but then it would extinguish as soon as he got it near my hair. He kept closing it, giving it a shake and trying it again – but it wouldn't stay alight. He was getting frustrated.

Then I saw the reason why he couldn't set light to my hair: the monk was leaning over me and blowing the lighter out. I couldn't understand what I was seeing – how could this be happening? I thought, oh no, I've really lost the plot now.

There was more. From the night of the rape, I'd had the clear memory of floating to the top of the wardrobe and sitting there, watching the boys raping me down below. That memory evolved too. Now I saw myself watching the scene with the monk sitting next to me. It was a bit surreal; we were both on top of the wardrobe, watching the scene below, which we were both in. I saw him cover my naked body with his shawl and comfort me, telling me over and over, 'It will all be OK.'

I started to get strange sensations during the day as well. One time, I was at my kitchen sink, doing the dishes, when a flash of burgundy cloth went past my window, the exact same colour as his robe. I went out the back door to see if anyone was there, but nobody was. Sometimes I'd feel cloth brush past my arm, always on my right side, but I'd see nothing there.

* * *

For many years, the memories in my dreams were too much and I'd awaken with a sudden fright, only to see Gerry and Randall's faces above me. But now I was seeing the monk too. I'd see him just standing by my bed, not saying a word. His presence calmed me.

At times, I could feel my hair and face being very lightly stroked, as if a spider had walked over them. But when I'd go to brush the spider away with my hand, there was never anything there.

On the one hand, I felt so disturbed by what I was dreaming, seeing and feeling, but on the other, I felt so comforted and protected. This went on for a good few months before I decided to bring it to my therapy sessions with Ron. By that time, I was convinced I was mad or making it up – or both –

and that this was the evidence I needed to present to Ron in order to confirm my insanity.

I was so nervous telling him; I was sure he would laugh at me and kick me out, but he didn't. Instead he sat there with a straight face as I told him about the young monk that I'd seen and felt, both awake and asleep. Much to my surprise, he didn't think I was mad at all – he just said that these things can happen. I clocked him to see if he was being serious; he wasn't laughing.

I asked him over and over again, how could this happen? Maybe I had made it all up; maybe my mind was finding a way to explain things that couldn't be explained or creating a story that was more elaborate and dramatic. He just calmly looked at me and asked, 'Why would you have made it up?' It was the same question he'd posed to me before, when I'd had the initial flashback memories during the residential weekend at college. Again, I couldn't find an answer.

I started to feel that there was something so familiar about the monk, as if he'd been around me for my entire life, but the instant that thought came into my mind, I'd tell myself I was really mad. There was a game of ping-pong going on in my head. Despite the reassurance Ron gave me, I needed to know once and for all: am I mad or is this real?

One time after a fire dance in Glasgow, I was crying during the Enya song when I felt a light tap on my shoulder: it was Amanda, one of the crew working for Emahó. 'Will you come with me?' she said, and she led me around the back of some screens to where Emahó was sitting on the steps to the stage. After motioning for me to sit next to him, he put my head on his lap, covered me up with his coat and gently stroked my hair over and over again while I cried.

I got so confused in that moment – it brought back so many familiar feelings of being comforted by the monk, and I wondered if Emahó had been the monk in a former life and if he had been with me that night when I was thirteen. When the song ended I stopped crying, sat up and started to tell him about my most recent dreams and experiences with the monk.

He told me that he wasn't my monk, but he said that I was very protected that night and, because I came so close to being killed, I got to see things that most people will never see. I got to see that there is a lot more going on in life than most people will ever know about. The severity of the situation opened doors in me that stay shut for the majority of the population.

His words soothed me and somewhere deep inside of me, they made sense too.

CHAPTER TWENTY-SEVEN

MEMORIES

The talk with Emahó helped put my mind at ease for a time, but I continued to struggle because the flood of memories just kept coming. And the more I complained to myself about them, the more strongly they flooded in. I realised that I had to find a way to accept them, or I would forever be in turmoil.

Someone at college told me they had seen a good medium, called Isobel, who used tarot cards and worked on the Victoria Road near me. I decided to make an appointment to see if she could help settle my mind; I wasn't going to give her any clues, I'd wait and see if she would come up with anything connected to that night on her own.

Not long into the session, she asked me if I wanted to hear anything, even if it was bad. I said yes, and she went on to ask me if I knew that I had been in danger of being killed by two men who weren't from this country when I was a young teenager. She said that I was taken to a room in an empty flat, where they tortured and raped me for many hours; that the room smelled of alcohol and pot. She described a scene where she saw Randall drag me from the flat to the stairwell, carry me to the landing and dangle me over the banister by my ankles. She said the other young man stopped him, but that wasn't the only outside influence that kept me alive: as soon as I went into that room, a Tibetan monk went in with me and helped prevent them from killing me.

I could not believe what I was hearing – I had not yet told anyone about getting dragged from the flat and dangled over the banister, even though I'd dreamt about that exact same thing over and over.

She also saw them burning me with their cigarettes and told me the exact locations on my body. Shocked at her accuracy, I started to get upset. I then thanked her and left abruptly, stunned by all that I had heard. It left me in a daze – and it gave me a lot to think about.

I had known for many years, through my work at Women's Aid and Rape Crisis, that the mind can shut out memories after a trauma, a bit like a safety valve. The mind does it as a means of protection; otherwise, the trauma of the memories could cause a serious breakdown, one that may not be curable. I had also heard many women saying that they'd felt themselves leave the scene of the crime by floating out of their body and observing what was being done to them. By having an out-of-body experience, the event feels dream-like, and, like a dream, it can be difficult to remember – until something triggers the memories to return.

When I thought about it, the triggers were obvious: the combination of the psychotherapy course and psychotherapy; attending Emahó's workshops; and the fact that my daughter Anna was about to turn thirteen, the age that I was when it all happened. When I looked at her, I saw a young, innocent girl and I couldn't imagine her going through what I had. It was always going to come back; it was just a question of timing.

It felt like I had numbed out for so many years, putting myself in a deep freeze, and now I was beginning to defrost. I had spent years trying to be the perfect wife and mother to cover up what had happened so that I could get on with my life. In many ways, I'd done that. There were times when I'd even managed to forget about it and put it to sleep – that sleep was over.

Remembering the details of all the many different ways they raped me was hard, but the hardest memory of all was when I saw Randall urinating on me. This summed up how little regard they'd had for me as a human being, and it left me feeling totally humiliated and degraded. And I know that this was the root cause for never feeling clean for years, and for hours trying to get their smell off me by scrubbing my body with cleaning products in the bath.

When I thought about all my many fears and phobias, I

knew something severe must have happened to me – they didn't feel 'normal'. Why was it that I couldn't let someone put his or her arms around my neck without feeling panicked? Or laugh at any sexual jokes or innuendos and instead get offended? Why could I never say the word 'rape', or even feel comfortable with my own kitchen knives? Why did I have such low self-esteem and such a poor self-image?

Then there was the list of my behaviours over the years: promiscuity, drugs and alcohol, not speaking, anorexia, suicide attempts, paranoia about safety, deep distrust of most men, extreme drop in performance at school, jumping at any noise I heard, locking the car doors, locking my front door as soon as I came home, not answering the front door if I didn't know who it was, fear of childbirth, fear of the dark, fear of male professionals, issues with sex, fear of injections, the hostile and sarcastic way I spoke to men, etc. And so the list went on and I knew it all had to have come from somewhere.

I was tired of all the fighting I had been doing with myself over the last three years, not knowing whether I could trust these memories or not. I'd been so identified by what had been done to me that somehow I felt what they did was a reflection on me. But I was beginning to see it differently now, even though I still had a lot of shame. When I looked at my thirteen-year-old daughter, it was clear that it would never be her fault if anybody hurt her in the same way.

I had to find a way to make peace with my past – I was, after all, not the sum of my memories. The more I slowly allowed myself to acknowledge what had been done to me, the more my mind started to calm down; the sting and the shock had been removed by the images I saw. I still didn't like them, but they no longer had such a strong effect on me. The triggers and memories had increasingly less hold over my body; physical responses during my sessions with Ron became less and less frequent.

The frequency of nightmares and flashbacks diminished until they eventually stopped. I also started to realise that I wasn't what was done to me; they only hurt my body and I was so much more than that. I wasn't even my mind that had confused me over the years. What *was* my mind anyway – was it real? If I could cut it open, there wouldn't be any blood. They could never touch the real essence of me, which was still burning inside, untouched. I saw that it was not that I'd forgotten what was done to me, just that I didn't want to remember.

CHAPTER TWENTY-EIGHT

TELLING STEVEN

During one of our sessions, Ron suggested that it would be a good idea for me to tell Steven the details of what had happened to me so that he could understand why the therapy had been going on for nearly three years now. I knew it was a good idea, but the thought of it scared me. Up until that point, only Ron knew all of the details, and I wasn't sure how Steven would react. My old feelings resurfaced: what if it changed something between us, if he was disgusted by it all?

I saw how Steven would study my face whenever I returned home from a college weekend or if I had been to a session that day. He could see it was hard work and that it left me emotionally drained, which was unusual for me. I normally wore a mask and pretended everything was OK, but I couldn't keep up the facade any more.

Recently there had been a change in our relationship. I no longer needed a couple of drinks or a puff or two of a joint to get me in the mood for sex. Using those substances had been my usual method of operation since my teenage years, and it hit me one night that the alcohol and pot created distance between Steven and me: it made our intimacy feel less real. Of course, that's why I started using them in the first place, but it took me some time to see that I'd outgrown the habit. And it was great! I became much more present in our lovemaking and it felt so much better, apart from one thing: I started to see the boys' faces again, and I thought to myself, 'Not now!' Why did they have to intrude and spoil this special and beautiful moment? After making love and while we were still holding each other, I would cry. It was like years before, but less extreme – these were gentle and painful tears that escaped my eyes.

Steven would ask me if I was OK; I'd assure him that I was, and then he would just hold me until the tears stopped. It got to the point where it happened every time we were intimate. He would just place his cheek against mine to feel for tears and hold me even tighter. This went on for about three years while I was in therapy. It saddened me, but Steven always reacted with so much support and I felt so loved by him. I may have cried every time, but I also thanked the universe for sending him to me every time, too.

Of course I knew Ron was right, I had to share what had happened to me so that Steven could really understand it all.

I tried to bring it up during the day, but I felt ashamed and couldn't look at him; I became worried I would never be able to do it. Finally, I told Steven what Ron had suggested and asked if he would be OK to hear it all. He replied yes. The light was green, but I still had to find the courage to do so.

One night we were in bed with the lights off, chatting about our day, and it hit me that this was the only way I could tell him: in the dark without looking at him. Steven knew I'd been for a session that day, and when he asked how it went, I knew it was time.

He held my hand while he listened. I managed to tell him all that I could remember, all the details of what they did to me that night. He was shocked, but steady. I started to cry when I said, 'They could have killed me.' He just replied, 'But they didn't.'

Steven was right, they hadn't killed me: I was alive and happily married to him, with three beautiful girls. In that moment I felt profound relief for having shared, but so much gratitude for my life, too.

CHAPTER TWENTY-NINE

ALL OF ONE NIGHT

Something changed inside me after I told Steven; I could feel a shift. It was as if the final, elusive piece of the puzzle, unfinished for so many years, had been put in place. It started the process of integrating all the new information with my mind and body. I no longer had anything to hide or run from.

The nightmares and dreams had stopped. I could watch the scenes in my mind without panicking and just accept them for what they were – simply memories. They had played over and over, like an endless loop in my head, but that had stopped too. It became peaceful inside me; the wars had ceased and I laid down all weapons that I had used against myself.

And finally, I could remember that night in its entirety rather than in bits and pieces, here and there. Perhaps there are some small details that are lost forever, but I know that when I decided to finally accept all of what I was shown over that three-year period, everything changed: the fighting and the questioning were over.

AUTHOR'S NOTE

During the process of writing this book, my editor and I had a lot of discussions about how much detail I should include about the rape. I was concerned for lots of reasons, but mainly my 'social mind' worried about what other people would think. After a lot of consideration, I decided that all the details should be included in order to paint a clear picture of what really takes place when someone is raped. However, in so doing, I need to put a warning here: this may be difficult to read if you too are a survivor or if someone close to you has endured such an assault. Some of the details have already been mentioned as partial memories, but they're included again, this time in full context. Between here and the end of the chapter is what I remember of that one night.

They put me on the floor of the bedroom. It was a wooden floor with a red, blue and cream-coloured Persian rug. I saw tassels from the bedcover hanging over the end of the bed. Gerry straddled me and took off my top, covered in vomit, and my bra. He was not gentle in the process. He started to fondle my breasts and commented to Randall, who was sitting on the bed, watching, that they were big and that my underarms needed a shave. He was laughing at me. I was smiling nervously at the time, as at that point I had no idea what was to follow, but Gerry saw my smile and said, 'Hey, she's enjoying herself!' Randall replied with something like, 'Then let's give her something to remember.'

Gerry pulled the rest of my clothes off until I was naked on the floor. He then felt up the rest of my body. He put his fingers inside me, then took my hand and made me rub his crotch over his trousers. I could feel his erection and I started to panic. I screamed and kicked and punched and yelled at him to leave me alone. Randall shot up from the bed, pushed Gerry away, straddled me and wrapped his hands around my neck, pressing his thumbs hard into the base of my throat, strangling me and banging my head hard against the floor, over and over. I felt panicky and sick; it was as if he was squeezing the life out of me. I wanted to scream, but I couldn't catch my breath. I felt very dizzy and everything was getting darker.

He spat in my face and brought his own face close to mine; he was screaming and swearing at me to shut up. He then punched me in the face and body. Afterwards he got up quickly and kicked me, with his boots on, hard between the legs. I felt the sharp pain of his blows, but what really struck me was the look in his eyes: it was clear that he was very dangerous and absolutely capable of killing me.

I also realised in that moment that I was lying on a carpet, completely naked and drunk, in a room with two boys I didn't know, who were becoming increasingly violent by the second, and no one – none of my family or friends – knew where I was. Panic and terror filled my being.

Gerry got back on top of me, pushing my shoulder against the floor while he unzipped his jeans and pulled them halfway down. I felt the heavy weight of his body, and his studded belt digging into the skin on my thighs. When he forced his penis into my vagina I experienced a pain like fire. I remember watching beads of sweat form on his forehead, roll down his face and then fly off into my own face as he moved back and forth. They were disgusting – and I couldn't avoid them. I carried on watching the drops of his sweat forming, rolling and flying, seemingly in slow motion, while he raped me. His breathing was so heavy and his head so close to me that I could feel his greasy hair flap in my face. His breath reeked of cigarettes. I could also smell his body odour, which was strong and stale, like he hadn't bathed or changed his T-shirt in days.

At the same time, I could hear people outside the window, down in the communal garden, having a party. I could smell their barbecue coming through the open window in the bedroom. It was a nice night outside and I could hear adults talking and children playing. I wondered what they were having to eat. It seemed surreal that both of these things were going on at the same time. I did my best to focus on the people and party outside, not the man on top of me. All of a sudden, I felt myself float out of my body and found myself gazing down at the scene on the floor below. It felt as though I was witnessing something happening to someone else, but then I'd sink back into my body and again see and feel and smell Gerry on top of me, grunting and sweating.

Then I found another distraction: the room had a wallpaper border with pink and grey bows around the tops of walls, and so I started to count the bows. Each section of the wall had eleven bows, and with four walls in the room, that made forty-four bows in total.

Somehow I hadn't noticed that Gerry had got off me. I looked up to see Randall straddling me. He pushed one of his hands into my shoulder to pin me down. Then he leaned down and got his face close to mine, silently staring into my eyes as he reached his other hand into his jacket pocket. With a flick of his wrist, the blade swung open. He pushed my chin back, put the knife to my throat and said if I didn't shut up, he would kill me. I knew he meant it. He then ran the knife all over my body, stopping at my breasts, pretending he was going to slice my nipples off. 'Should I cut them off? *Should I?*' he asked.

He then said to Gerry, 'Let's give her something to scream about again.' They turned me over and put me on to all fours. I could hear and feel him spitting against my anus. Then I felt a shot of searing pain as he inserted himself into me. He grabbed hold of my buttocks, digging his nails in – I thought my body was going to be split in two. Then Gerry got on his knees, facing me, and forced his penis into my mouth at the same time. He was pulling my hair and ramming his penis into my mouth with such force that I gagged and threw up, but he didn't pull out. I could feel him hit the back of my throat and was aware of his pubic hair around my mouth. They were both raping me, anally and orally, at the same time. Gerry ejaculated into my mouth; they high-fived each other. The texture and the taste of his semen made me sick again. Randall carried on raping me anally, grabbing onto my hair and pulling my head back until he too ejaculated.

As I collapsed onto the floor, I started to cry, begging them to leave me alone. Randall sat down on the bed and lit up a joint. 'Shut up, bitch! Shut up, whore!' he kept shouting at me. He got up from the bed, grabbed the cigarette that Gerry was smoking and used it to burn my breasts, the insides of my thighs and the bottoms of my legs. He kicked me several more times. All the while Gerry was laughing.

He barked at Gerry to get something to tie me up with. I could hear him rifle through drawers until he came over with some tights he'd found. They tied my right wrist and right ankle to the radiator pipes.

Then it was as if they took a party break. The room stank of pot and cigarettes. They drank beers and popped some pills and acted as though I weren't there. Exhausted and terrified, I watched them from the floor.

Gerry was drinking a beer when Randall seized the bottle from his hand. He came over to me and inserted it into my vagina and raped me with it. I felt my body tear, but then he took it out, inserted it the other way and continued raping me. They were both laughing.

Randall pulled the bottle out and put some of his fingers inside me. He took them out and licked the blood off them, looking me in the eye as he did so. Then he put all of his fingers and then his fist inside me. He had a ring on his finger, and every time he drew his fist in and out of me, I could feel the ring tearing my skin. Gerry handed him a chocolate bar and he inserted it into me. Again he pulled it out and licked the blood off it. He did this many times until he ate it, close up to my face.

When he'd finished the chocolate bar, Randall started punching me again. He stood up and kicked me some more, but I couldn't figure out why, because I had stopped fighting against them and I wasn't making any more sounds. He knelt down on the floor next to me, took out a silver Zippo lighter and grabbed hold of my hair. 'Let's burn the bitch, set her on fire!' he was saying. Over and over, he tried to set my hair alight, but the lighter kept going out as soon as it got close to me. He kept closing and flicking the top of the lighter open, trying over and over again. A flame would appear, he'd move the lighter to my hair but then it would go out.

It was at this point that I became aware of a young monk in a burgundy robe and an orange shawl sitting by my right side in between me and the radiator I was tied to. He was about twenty years old, with short, black hair. I couldn't explain how I knew, but I thought him to be Tibetan. His robe was like a long dress with no collar or sleeves, and had thin blue borders around the hems at his upper arms. There were two orange triangles on the front of the robe and an orange square on the back. He was blowing the lighter out. Every time it got close to my hair, he would lean across me and blow it out.

I became aware that I had floated out of my body again, and this time I felt as if I was sitting on top of the wardrobe, observing the scene of Randall trying to set my hair alight and the monk blowing out the flame. And yet the monk was by my side on the wardrobe, watching the scene as well. It felt very surreal, sitting on the wardrobe with the monk, seeing myself tied up on the floor with him by my side. The monk was quietly telling me I was going to be OK, and he was covering up my naked body with his orange shawl. He sat there on the floor next to me, praying and chanting.

Frustrated with his lighter, Randall got back on top of me and inserted himself into my vagina, raping me again. But I was so numb by now that I couldn't feel the pain of it anymore. He came, but wasn't finished: he flicked open his knife again and stabbed me inside my vagina. I felt more blood trickling down my thighs. This time I thought that he would kill me: there was a dark, cold, hollow look in his eyes, and it felt like there was nothing behind them.

Gerry was screaming at him, asking him, 'What have you done? Why did you do *that*?' But Randall just laughed.

After that, I remember the boys left the room for some time while the monk, still by my side, comforted me. I remember wanting to be killed to make it all stop, wishing they'd just get it over with so it could end.

I don't know how long they were gone, but when they came back in, Randall noticed that I had urinated and he laughed, saying, 'Look at her, she's pissed herself!' Then he undid his trousers, took his penis out of his underwear and urinated over my body. Gerry bent down and pulled my mouth open so he could get it in my mouth. I shook my head, trying to get out of the way, but then he stamped on my head to keep it still and Randall managed to get it in my mouth. They laughed as I coughed and spluttered, trying to get air. Out of everything they did to me, I don't know why but this felt the worst. It was one of the images that haunted me for a long time, more than anything else. I think it just summed up how little regard they had for another human, and it made me feel utterly worthless and totally degraded.

Then Randall said, 'Let's finish the bitch off.' He untied my ankle and wrist from the radiator and dragged me by my legs out of the room, banging my head on the doorway. Then he opened the front door and picked me up, carrying me out to the landing. He put me down, picked me up by the ankles and dangled me over the banister (we were four floors up). I fully believed he was going to drop me when Gerry started to scream at him, telling him to stop, saying, 'We can't kill her!' He managed to talk him out of it. I remember again floating above my body, watching Randall hold me out above the stairwell.

Randall brought me back over the banister and dropped me on the landing. I remember Gerry picking me up and carrying me, quite gently now, but also being aware that the monk was carrying me too and speaking to Gerry, who didn't see or hear him.

They took me back into the same bedroom, putting me on the bed this time, and I nearly fell out. At this, Gerry laughed and said, 'She wants some more!'

Randall looked menacingly at me then tugged my hair, punched me in the chest a few times and held the knife to my throat again, telling me that if I ever told anyone about what had happened, he would find me and kill me. I believed him. He was arguing with Gerry that he should have let him finish me off, but Gerry said, 'No, she won't talk.' And with that they left. The monk sat cross-legged on the floor next to the bed, praying and chanting.

* * *

This is as much as I remember of what they did to me. There may have been other details – I drifted in and out of consciousness from the alcohol and the pain and I left my body several times. I can't say exactly how long the whole thing lasted, but I'd estimate three to five hours. It was shocking for me to have all the details back, but reassuring too as it helped make sense of how I had behaved over the years and why.

CHAPTER THIRTY

FORGIVENESS

I never set out to forgive the men who raped me, quite the opposite. I wanted them to not just experience the pain and humiliation of what they did to me, but for them to fully understand that the suffering doesn't stop after one night, that it goes on affecting one's life in countless ways. I'm not very proud to admit it, but I fantasised about someone kidnapping them, tying them up, beating them up, and raping and torturing them for hours on end, just like they had done to me. I wanted them to know how scarred they had left me.

I looked at them as an evil pair of animals, not really human at all. But something happened to me in therapy, which started to shift my perception of them. Ron suggested to me, near to the end of my three years in therapy, that perhaps they didn't come into this world as rapists; that maybe something made them change into what they became.

I was outraged! Did he want me to start feeling sorry for them? They were evil and sadistic, and as far as I was concerned that was it. I went from trying to grasp what he was saying to hating them, and getting angry over and over again in the process. But he had planted a seed in my mind, and very slowly it took root and began to grow.

Emahó came to Glasgow soon after that therapy session and I went along to his workshop. In his teaching, he talked about how we are all born into this world as a blank sheet. The things that take place in our lives change that: as we become conditioned to our surroundings and experiences, we act accordingly. I couldn't believe my ears; I had always thought that they must have been born evil, and now Emahó, in different words, was saying the same thing that Ron was saying.

I started to wonder: if this were true, what had happened to them? What had they witnessed or experienced that taught them how to be so violent with another human being at such a young age?

A friend of mine used to be a midwife, and she told me that she had brought thousands of babies into this world, but had never met an evil one. That had always stayed with me, and I could hear her words going round and round my mind.

Despite not wanting to, I found myself thinking about their predicament a lot. Hating them as I did kept me feeling angry, and even though I was doing so much better, I could see I still had issues. I could never completely relax; I was obsessed with keeping things tidy and everything being in its place. With my family, I was still uptight and a bit snappy at times, and not very spontaneous; I still felt I had to be in control. Was that what holding onto the hatred was doing to me? It was leaking out, poisoning my family – and me.

I wondered how they could live with themselves after what they had done to me, and I feared for other women, too. In time, I realised that whether they were consciously aware of it or not, it would leak out into their lives, one way or another, and their actions would ultimately cause them more harm than they had inflicted upon me. I was really turning things around and felt so grateful to be alive. But I wasn't so sure about them. I started to dream about them, and in my dreams I saw Randall getting killed by his own knife in a street fight. I saw Gerry in prison, a convicted sex offender. I'll never know if this is true – I've never tried to find out what happened to them, and I never heard from Kelly again after leaving school. But I didn't imagine they were in a good space after what they had done to me; it had to have affected them in some way.

Slowly I realised that as my understanding grew, my compassion also expanded. I was starting to forgive them, something I'd never thought possible years before. It became clear that for me, forgiveness was the only way. If I continued to hold on to my anger towards them, they wouldn't have any idea and I'd be keeping myself in a prison. I saw the futility and destruction of my anger.

I'd had many surprises and revelations along the way to healing, but this, forgiveness, really caught me off guard. And yet I could see clearly that it was the only one that made sense. Forgiveness has freed me of any negative feelings towards them or myself, but more importantly, it has brought peace.

I realise that some may see forgiveness as weakness, as letting them off, but I disagree. I found that it's easy to stay angry, but it takes a lot of courage to face and overcome so many difficult emotions that can last for a lifetime, if one looks the other way. The desire for vengeance is ultimately draining.

Initially, I had to forgive myself and lose any blame before I could forgive them. It took me time to see that I was simply a young, naïve girl who trusted people to get me home safely. That understanding has transformed me.

I can honestly say that I no longer have any feelings of hate, anger or revenge in my heart towards them. It's a huge relief to have let all that go and it's a much freer way to live my life.

CHAPTER THIRTY-ONE

THROUGH THE BODY

While I was at college, I learned how important it was for me to incorporate my body alongside psycho-therapy, and this made a lot of sense. The list of physical evidence of trauma in my body was lengthy: jumpiness, an inability to relax, immediate tension resulting from distrust for no reason, panic reactions to mundane occurrences, and a nearly constant pit of anxiety in my stomach. Not only that, it was also clear to me that I operated from my head most of the time. I knew that because my mind was consumed with thoughts of worry and was constantly analysing situations for my safety; I could go on like that and survive, but not really live.

Not long after I had started therapy, someone suggested I see a woman called Caroline, who did therapeutic massage and cranial sacral therapy. Since she was based at my college and often used one of the tutors' rooms in the basement to do her treatments, it was almost too convenient not to see her. Still, I felt self-conscious having a massage at college; I worried that someone would walk in and see me in a semi-undressed state. I could hear voices outside the room and that only added to my irrational concern.

I got undressed to my underwear, climbed up onto the massage table and laid down on my back. She covered my torso and most of my legs with a towel. Caroline worked in an instinctive way and would address an area of the body that she felt guided to. I appreciated the spontaneity of her work; somehow it seemed more personal than if someone was just going through the paces of their routine.

In our first session, I was lying on my back while she massaged my shoulders, when she put both her hands around my neck. I started to hear someone screaming and shouting 'Get off!' and 'Don't kill me!' and then I realised it was me. I was startled by my own reactions. My arms and legs were flailing about as if I was fighting someone off, and my hands, formed into fists, were banging the massage table. This all came straight from my body.

I felt so embarrassed. I apologised because I'd unintentionally hit her with one of my flailing arms. She reassured me it was OK and she carried on. The next thing I knew, my shoulders had started to tremble; the trembling flowed into both my arms and, within moments, I was shaking all over, right down to my toes. As I covered my face up from more embarrassment,

I felt a wave of shame rising up inside me. I cried so much even my ears filled up with tears.

She just held onto my feet, trying to ground me, and reassured me that it was OK, that I needn't worry about the shaking or the tears. When the shaking and crying stopped, I told her that I had just started therapy and was worried that I couldn't trust the memories that were coming in. 'Could I have made them up?' I asked. Without hesitation she said no. To Caroline, and to Ron, my memories were simply my memories. Neither of them could see any reason why I would make up such things. I didn't know why I would either; I don't know that anyone would classify me as 'dramatic' and I certainly wasn't looking for any attention. But I still wasn't entirely convinced at that point.

And so I decided to look at it differently. I couldn't rely on my mind, but my body gave me plenty of evidence that those things really happened to me. My mind had nothing to do with it. When I did react, my first thoughts were to wonder what was going on! It made no sense that I would make all this up.

Caroline also explained how our emotions get stuck within our bodies, embedded deep within the cells of our muscles. If we don't deal with them, there they will stay. As much as I found it uncomfortable, I knew it was important for me to carry on with the bodywork to help clear out the trauma trapped inside me. Caroline was facilitating the release of it. Initially, it left me exhausted, but after a few more sessions I felt lighter as emotions were shifted and released.

I went to her for five years and had many different reactions in the sessions, ranging from shaking to crying to throwing up. Several times, I could feel their hands around my neck, choking me again, and I coughed violently, trying to get air. One day, Caroline told me that she had to work inside my mouth and that it might be uncomfortable, but I trusted her and said, 'Sure, do it.' The pain was excruciating and the tears I felt came from such a deep place inside me, which was hard, but it reassured my mind that my reactions were genuine.

I remember how effective the breath work was at college, but we weren't doing that much of it in my psychotherapy year, so I decided to try and do some research and find someone in Glasgow that I could go to. I came across the website of Alan Dolan, who did what he described as 'transformational breath work'. He lived in Lanzarote, but came to Glasgow a few times a year to do one-to-one sessions. I got a good sense from him when I studied his photo, so I sent an email to make an appointment for the next time he would be in Glasgow.

The fact that he worked at a friend's flat in the West End of the city gave me little solace; I still wasn't comfortable working with men and even less so when it wasn't in a professional setting. But this man had a good reputation so I refused to let those concerns keep me away.

I found the flat and was greeted by a laid-back looking guy with a friendly smile, who invited me in. It was a nice flat and that helped ease my mind a bit. But when he led me to his workspace in one of the bedrooms, I started to panic. I managed to find my voice and express my fears, telling him that I was uncomfortable because I didn't know him and that I would be alone with him in a bedroom. I could see that my objections didn't bother him in the slightest as he kindly turned and told me not to worry because he was gay.

He asked me a few general questions, but never enquired as to why I had come for a session. He then invited me to lie face up on the double bed, while he sat cross-legged up on the bed behind me. Just having him on the bed behind me put me in a panic but I fought the wave of it. As he took me through the steps of his transformational breath work technique, it became very apparent that for probably the vast majority of my life, I'd only been taking shallow breaths. It was as if I'd been holding my breath for years.

He laid his hand on my chest and stomach, encouraging me to breathe deeper and to feel both areas filling and rising with air. Then he placed a large tube in my mouth to help open it wider so I could get more oxygen. I soon settled into the rhythm of the breath that he was guiding me to, and started to get strange sensations in my hands.

It began with intense pins and needles, and then my fingers started to curl tightly into fists. I tried to open them, but I couldn't; my hands were frozen, paralysed. I also felt the same pattern of wanting to fight him off, but I resisted it. Seeing my struggle, Alan reassured me it was OK, that it was just old fear.

Again I tried to open my hands but I couldn't. It disarmed me to see how much I was holding on to fear and again to see how strongly my body reacted without any obvious external triggers. And again, it showed me that these reactions were not purely in my head, not by a long stretch. It made me wonder: how much was I holding myself back with all this fear operating inside me?

It was clear that even though Alan was gay, I still had a considerable fear of being alone with a strange man, gay or not. But his genuine care allowed my fears to fade and leave my body. He never once asked about the root of my fear, he just supported and guided me with each breath. After a long while, my fingers relaxed to the point where I could move them, and I let go even more. When they finally opened, releasing their fierce grip, I shook them and shook them, trying to restore the blood flow and ease the stiffness.

As I carried on, a sense of peacefulness came into my breath that I hadn't experienced for a long time. I saw that whatever had been done to me, the essence of me was still there and that it could never be touched by anything ever done to me. In that moment I became even more determined to do whatever it took to build on that feeling and nurture the fire I felt in my belly. I felt a connection to something no physical or mental trauma could disturb.

Over the next few years, I saw Alan whenever he came to Glasgow, and each time the fear lessened and the joy in me grew. There was more space inside me, more space for the me who hadn't been raped; I was starting to feel energised and alive. The breath work showed me that I could clean up what was buried deep inside me and that I could take my body to a very relaxed state of letting go. I felt like I was in a lift, sinking lower and lower into myself, beyond all the events of my life, to a stillness and quiet I can only describe as profound.

CHAPTER THIRTY-TWO

THAWING

What on earth is a sweat lodge? That was my first thought when I heard that our college class would be doing one; I had never heard of such a thing and had no idea what it was. One Saturday morning, we all drove to a field in Cockston, just outside Glasgow, to meet Liz, who would be leading us in the lodge. I learned that a sweat lodge is a Native American tradition whereby one purifies through sweating. OK, purification sounded good. The lodge itself looked like an igloo and was made from branches that had been bent and tied into shape. We were invited to help with the finishing touches by spreading blankets over the lodge to completely cover it: it had to be totally dark inside.

The thought of being in the dark was not in the least bit alluring: quite the contrary, it put me in a mild panic. But I wanted to try and stay with it and give it a go. I voiced my concerns to Liz; she said to stay by her when we went inside and that I could always go out if I wanted to.

She had an assistant, or fire-keeper, who tended to a large fire. Cooking in the fire were many large stones that had been in there for a few hours, getting good and hot. We all stood around the fire, mesmerised, as one gets sitting by a campfire. And the heat felt really nice! Liz told us that the stones were ready now, that it was time to get changed. I was a bit embarrassed by seeing everyone strip down right then and there so I found a tree to get changed behind. The women wore sarongs and the men wore shorts.

The fire-keeper ran the smoke from a piece of burning sage over us (another Native American form of purification); we walked around the outside of the lodge a few times to quieten our minds, and then crawled into the lodge on our hands and knees through a small door where some blankets were folded back. I went in last and positioned myself behind Liz: if need be, I could make an easy escape through the door right next to me.

The fire-keeper brought the hot stones in one at a time on a garden fork and slowly lowered each of them into a pit in the centre of the lodge. They actually glowed red – I'd never seen stones glow before. After ten stones were brought in, the fire-keeper pulled the blankets down to close the door, and with the exception of the very dim glow of the rocks, everything fell into complete darkness. I couldn't even see my hand in front of me. I started to panic; my instinct was to get the hell out of there.

Liz must have sensed my panic because she reached back to hold my hand. It helped and kept me from running. She told me to focus on my breath. Then she let go of my hand and poured water over the stones, which made a loud, crackling sound and created a lot of hot steam inside the lodge. The temperature instantly shot up.

As Liz poured more water on the stones and the temperature in the lodge continued to rise quickly, a lot of people started moaning about the heat. I felt it, but that wasn't an issue: the darkness was my big challenge. When she had stopped pouring, she picked up her drum and started to sing what I imagine was a Native American song. The drum and song spoke to my bones and calmed me. Liz then called for the fire-keeper to open the door – it was the end of the first 'round'. The blankets were folded back, light poured in and steam flooded out. But we stayed in place as the fire-keeper brought in ten more stones and the next round began; we did three rounds in all.

I couldn't believe that I had stayed with it all despite feeling so scared. I was starting to see that while I felt fear, it didn't stop me from doing things if I didn't indulge the urge to run. It showed me that if I just held on, despite the fear, I could find a way through it. I found myself asking Liz to tell me when she would have the next sweat lodge – that was the first of many sweat lodges for me.

For some time, I struggled to feel the heat no matter where I sat in the lodge or how many stones were brought in. Everyone else was lying on the ground, trying to get cool, while I sat upright, hardly sweating at all. So Liz suggested that I kneel by the stone pit in the centre of the lodge and cover myself with a towel, creating a kind of one-woman sweat lodge within a sweat lodge.

Then it hit me: by numbing out over the years, I had stopped feeling, not just emotionally but physically too. And the more my journey of therapy and various body treatments deepened, the more I started to defrost. Slowly, over time, I started to feel the heat from the stones. It amazed me how powerful the body/mind connection could be and also how shut-off and numb I really was. I'd not only shut myself off, but I'd also stopped people connecting with the real me as I was so held back. This started to change, and I began to trust more and open up with my family and friends.

Within time, I not only grew used to being in the dark, but I even came to find it comforting. Like a blanket wrapping itself securely around me, I felt held and supported by it. I was also learning that the more I went into things that scared me, the less they did so. Over the years I visited about forty sweat lodges in Scotland and it really helped to ground me and connect me to the earth, but more importantly, it also helped connect me to myself.

CHAPTER THIRTY-THREE

FACING FEARS

Over the course of so many years, I'd worked hard to understand, process and transcend the events from one night that had drastically changed the direction of my life. I had three beautiful daughters, worked as a volunteer to help women who had been the victims of violence, gained a degree in psychotherapy and been through years of therapy and body work, but still, two major obstacles remained. So far, nothing I'd done had truly taken away my fears about men and of being out of control.

If I looked at my life like a big house, I could see I'd worked hard for so many years to inspect every square inch, to find the messes and clean them up. I realised these fears were like the last room to clean before I could be at peace with my house, with what had happened to me, with my life. I had learned from therapy that the way in was the way out for me; only by facing it all could I really understand, process and ultimately come to terms with what happened to me.

I asked myself, what's fear anyway? Two acronyms came to mind: False Evidence Appearing Real and Face Everything And Rise. I had heard these many years before, and used both as reminders whenever I felt strong bolts of fear. But did I really want fear to walk alongside me for the rest of my life? I decided we'd been roommates in my body and mind for far too long and it was time to give notice of eviction.

It was clear to me that my fears held me back from really living and enjoying my life; they kept me more in my mind, always analysing a situation for safety and strategising an escape plan, if necessary. But why should I do that when there was no real danger? By worrying about what had happened to me in my distant past, I was worrying about what was going to happen next in my present life. Then it hit me: I suddenly realised my fears didn't really exist, that they were all coming from my memories and imagination.

During one of his teachings, Emahó said that fear is a very old entity, something that serves a specific purpose: it comes to aid people when their lives are in danger. It answers a silent call that people put out, comes in, does its job and leaves. It gets the adrenaline pumping and helps us get ourselves out of imminent danger. It's impossible for fear to remain in one's body; what remains are the memories of the fear, but not the actual fear itself. Emahó's words now made more sense than ever.

And so I decided I wanted to start living more in reality, more in the present time, in order to feel alive and enjoy my life. I felt that I was the one sabotaging myself, always holding myself back, by constantly keeping the events of the past fresh and active in my daily life: it was time for this to stop.

The fears, or memories of them, kept me restricted and imprisoned. They also defined me: but I'm not just a woman who has been raped, I'm much more than that. And yet I was so conditioned, so programmed by my experience, that it affected all aspects of my life. I felt determined to break this and lift all of the veils that clouded my decisions, all my perceptions of life. I began to wake up to the fact that I was not just made up of one experience; everything made me, all the events of my life made me the woman I am.

All these years, I had been so concerned with my safety and protection that I was protecting myself from living, too. I asked myself, did I want to carry on avoiding many aspects of life or did I want to start experiencing life?

First, I made the decision to find ways to get more comfortable around men. After all these years, all men were still potential threats to me. Time to end that. Next, I wanted to act spontaneously, to do things out of the ordinary without wondering if men would be present, if I would be by myself, if it would be dark outside, if I'd have to take public transport, or if I'd be in a new situation. I wanted to live free from the gravitational pull of my memories; I longed to discover what it meant to be more carefree and living in the now.

I realised that most of my fears were about what *could* happen and not what had already happened to me in the past. The worst thing imaginable to most women had already happened to me. It was as if I were constantly trying to close the stable door after the horse had bolted.

But I had survived it, and it wasn't happening to me anymore. I was determined to get past this once and for all, not just for me, but for my children as well. I'd shown them what it was to survive something, now it was time to show them what it was to live a full life. Because if I continued to carry fear around like ugly baggage chained to my wrist, it could easily transfer to them — and then what would have been the point of bringing three children into this world? I wanted them to be confident and independent and it was up to me to set that example.

Looking back, I cringe to myself thinking about when Anna started high school. I gave her a rape alarm for her pocket — what kind of message was that? I wanted to drive her to school every day, but she insisted on taking the bus, so despite feeling scared for her, I let her do that. She didn't know that I used to follow behind the bus in my car to make sure she got there safely. This had to stop.

CHAPTER THIRTY-FOUR

MY PARENTS

I often wonder if I survived what happened to me in the way that I did because of the family I was born into and the parents I had. Both of my parents overcame major life issues too, and showed me, by the ways in which they lived their lives, what was possible.

My mum got whiplash from a car accident when she was eighteen. As the years since the accident progressed, so too did numbness and pins and needles in her right hand and arm. After seeing her doctor, she was told she needed an X-ray to determine what was going on. However, Mum had a more pressing health concern. She had been diagnosed with ovarian cancer and needed an emergency hysterectomy, so the issues from the accident were put on hold until after the operation. But when she woke up from it, she was terrified to discover that she couldn't use her right hand at all.

She was kept in hospital while they investigated. The orthopaedic doctor determined that what she had was nerve damage, and used an electronic traction machine to pull her head and straighten her spine. Not surprisingly, it was too painful and they had to stop the treatment.

Her family doctor then referred her to a neurologist, who discovered that she had fractured vertebrae in her neck and two ruptured discs, which would need surgery to correct. No one would admit exactly how this had happened, but they believed it had occurred during the hysterectomy: her neck hadn't completely healed from the car accident, and the surgery had only made things much worse. She was diagnosed with brachial neuralgia, a condition marked by the swelling of the nerves that control the shoulder, arm and hand. Her case was extreme and required surgery. It was mostly successful, alleviating the pain in her arm and shoulder, but did little for her hand.

We would spend a lot of time in my mum's bedroom when she wasn't feeling well, to cheer her up and distract her from her hand. I remember one day we were listening to the radio with her, when a segment came on that was all about removing pain from the body using hypnosis and the power of the mind. It sounded truly fascinating and didn't involve any more surgeries, so we urged her to get in touch with the radio show to make an appointment to see the hypnotherapist, a man called Joe Keeton. She sent a letter to the station, which they forwarded on to Joe. As luck would have it, he was coming down to London in the next few days from the Wirral in north-west England.

Mum picked Joe up from the train station, brought him back to the house and fed him lunch – she's a good mother! He did hypnosis on her, but she came out of the trance a few times and it didn't really work on her. Joe told her that he'd be doing past life regression work over the weekend and asked her to come. It sounded interesting to her and she wanted to give hypnosis another go.

Not only did she go to his workshop over the weekend, she fell under hypnosis while Joe was performing it on someone else! And this time she went much deeper than before. Joe brought her out and then started a new session just for her. Under hypnosis, he asked her to notice the pain in her hand and told her that when she woke up, the pain would be gone. And it worked, mostly: when she came out of the session, the pain was almost entirely gone, diminished to a point that she had previously only achieved through medication. He then taught her self-hypnosis, to control the pain in the future.

For years, my mum had been telling me that she was fed up with lying in bed, feeling unwell. Life was passing her by, she felt, and she wasn't actively participating in it. And so she used her strong will and intention to fight back and heal herself: when she came home from that hypnosis session, she threw out all of her pain medicine in case she became tempted to use it. She was determined to make hypnosis work, and it did: she never used the painkillers again.

My dad was a Holocaust survivor from former Czechoslovakia. During World War II, in 1939, German soldiers physically forced him and his family from their home in Vulchovce and relocated them to a ghetto in Warsaw, Poland, where they lived for fifteen months. My grandfather managed to bribe some guards and they got back to their house, but it was only a three-year reprieve; in 1944, German soldiers came again and took them away for good, this time to Auschwitz. Without the soldiers noticing, my grandfather hid my dad in a kitchen cupboard. Dad remained there, silent, for several hours until he emerged and found himself completely alone.

For several months he hid in the house, moving below the view of the windows and only cooking at night. One neighbour helped by bringing him food so he could stay out of sight as much as possible, but another neighbour told the police he was there – harbouring a Jew was a criminal offence. Sure enough, the police pulled him from the house and sent him to a labour camp in Hungary, where he worked on building and improving roads in the area under very difficult conditions – my dad was only sixteen at the time.

One day, upon hearing an air raid siren, my dad decided he had had enough. After ripping the yellow star from his jacket, he ran. He hid during the day and kept running at night. He ate apples from the trees and drank milk from the cows in the fields.

There are so many details about his escape and life that I will never know, because he shut a lot off as his way of coping and rarely spoke of it. But we do have a photo of him at home, dressed in a Hitler Youth uniform, something he did for a while to blend in and hide in plain sight. He told me he was scared to pee in front of anyone – they might see he was circumcised, and therefore a Jew. Eventually he made his way to Budapest, where the Red Cross provided him with false papers. So my father, Leopold Gedajlovic (Leo Geddy to us), became Safar Lagos for the rest of the war. He posed as a Christian, lived in a hostel and went out with the housekeeper's daughter.

Dad had an amazing ability for languages and could speak four of them at the time: Yiddish, German, Hebrew and Czech. After the war, he learned English, French, Italian and Spanish. When he arrived in Budapest, he could speak only a few words of Hungarian or Russian. Within a few months, his command of both was good enough that he found work as an interpreter.

Russian soldiers liberated Budapest at the end of the war. When they came to the house where my father lived, he told them that he was Jewish. Then, when his housekeeper heard that she had been boarding a Jew *and* that he was going out with her daughter, she fainted.

It was not until after the war that my dad discovered his parents and most of his brothers and sisters had been murdered at Auschwitz. His youngest brother, Mordechai, was only six when he died in the camp. He also found out from friends and neighbours that his sister, Eva, had survived, so he went in search of her. But when he found her, the experience in the camp had already destroyed her: schizophrenia, agoraphobia and paranoia had left her a shadow of her former self. Still, he took her with him to Paris in search of a better life. When my father learned they had a brother living in London, they made their final move there.

Dad's story is classic rags-to-riches material: he arrived with nothing but the clothes on his back and built up a successful business in wholesale fashion jewellery. Then he met my mum, fell in love and they had the five of us. Sadly, he passed away in 1998. What people most remember about him was his love of life and his wicked sense of humour. The majority who knew him never had any idea what he had gone through – he felt there was no need for them to know. He always told me that life was for living, not for dwelling in the past.

Recently I read a book called *Supersurvivors: The Surprising Link Between Suffering and Success* by David B. Feldman and Lee Daniel Kravetz. The main message of the book, that it's what we do with what happened to us rather than what happened itself, completely resonated with me. When I finished the book, I contacted the authors to ask if there was any research linking genetics to survival and resilience.

Mr Kravetz responded, saying that it was an interesting question but no research had been done in that area. However, he also said that there is research pointing to the power of narrative. That is, if we know something very bad happened to someone we know and love, and that he or she survived it, often we tell ourselves that we, too, can survive and bounce back when bad things happen to us. To me, that made perfect sense. When I was struggling as a teenager, I would tell myself that if my dad could survive all that had happened to him, surely I could survive one night? The strength, courage and dignity my parents embodied shaped me, and for that, I am eternally grateful.

My mum still has pain in her right hand, but she never complains about it and just gets on with her life. It takes the same amount of energy to be miserable as it does to be happy. Dad never let the label of 'Holocaust survivor' define who he was. I often wonder if I would have survived had I been born into a different family, one without so much love of life to provide a narrative.

CHAPTER THIRTY-FIVE

WINDSURFING

As a family, we were very sporty and liked to go away on active holidays. No idle sitting on a beach for us! There was something for everyone in my family – lots of watersports, cycling, yoga, and kids' and teens' clubs.

In the summer of 2003, we went on our first 'sporty' holiday in Greece. Steven and I signed up for dinghy-sailing lessons. We laughed a lot, but I wasn't very good at it and I felt there were too many things to deal with. Besides that, I kept getting bashed on the head by the boom. So I decided to try windsurfing: there was only a board and a sail, how hard could it be? I went along to the first class, taught by a young guy, and quickly ascertained that I was the only woman. My first impulse was to flee, but I was determined to use every opportunity I could find to work through my issues surrounding men and being out of control. This gave me a chance to work on both at the same time in a safe environment: perfect.

Our first lesson was on land, going over where to stand, how to position your feet, how to turn around and working with the direction of the wind. Again, it sounded pretty easy. Then we got into the water and reality hit me like a prizefighter: it was so much harder than it looked! I struggled to even stand up on the board, let alone sail it.

When I did eventually stand up, every time I pulled the sail up, I fell in. I spent more time in the water than on my board. I was so preoccupied with trying to get the sail up and get moving that I hadn't noticed I had drifted out to sea. This panicked me; I felt far away from the shore, isolated and possibly in danger.

I gathered my thoughts and remembered being taught how to lie down on the board with the sail behind me and swim it in. Or we could wave to a safety boat and they would come and get us. OK, I have options, I thought. However, the wind had suddenly and drastically changed during my time on the water, causing a lot of boats to capsize. This was no gentle breeze.

I sat on my board and gave the signal to ask for help; I was so tired from constantly falling in and trying to right my sail that I was too exhausted to paddle myself into shore. But no one saw me because they were dealing with the capsized boats. I waited for ages and still no one came to get me; all the while, I was drifting further out to sea. That was when it hit me: I'm going to have to do this myself.

So I lay down on my board, directed it towards the water-front and, very slowly, I made my way in. My God, I couldn't even tell if I was moving any closer to the shore, but I kept on paddling! By the time I got back, the exhaustion in my arms was matched only by the relief of feeling the beach underneath my feet. I couldn't get over how the wind had changed so quickly from being a gentle breeze, ideal for beginners, to the gale-force winds that had forced the staff to close the water-front and get everyone out of the water.

My first introduction to windsurfing had been mayhem. Feeling out of control is one thing, but endangering my life is another, so I was scared to get back in the water. But hadn't I been doing the safe things all my life? I found some courage and forced myself to go back the next day.

Luckily, the wind was much kinder to me on the second day, but that didn't stop the butterflies in my stomach and the shaking in my legs when we got back in the water. Why was I doing this again? I kept on dropping the sail and having the same difficulties as the day before, spending ages in the water, getting tired and frustrated. The further I drifted out, the darker and deeper the water got, which also scared me. Something had to change. I started to realise that being so tense didn't help at all and that I had to find a way to relax.

My determination kicked in and I gave myself a good talking to. I pulled the sail up, got my feet and hands into the correct position, looked towards the direction that I wanted to sail to and started to move. And move I did! There was a lot of talking aloud to myself and, as I started to go faster, more than a wee bit of swearing. Then I heard a familiar voice in my head, sounding the warning: 'You're going too fast and you're out of control!' But that was exactly what I wanted. So rather than engage in a lengthy discussion with myself, I started to sing. It made a huge difference: I made it across the bay by myself without falling in, singing the entire way. Not only that, I turned the board around, changed direction and headed across again.

The more I learned to relax, the easier it became. Yes, I still fell in a lot, but I was able to get back up and right my sail with greater efficiency each time. I still felt panic as I got nearer to the rocks, wondering if I would manage to turn round OK, but I always got myself out of danger and soon I could go back and forth across the bay without ever falling. It felt like a great achievement.

I spent the rest of my holiday going to my course in the mornings and practising in the afternoons. Each time out I managed to sail more and more. My goal was to sail out and get back in without being rescued by the safety boat, and by the end of the holiday I managed to do just that.

It was a great holiday, and being on the board really helped me believe in myself. When I learned to relax and put my fears to one side, I was confident. Even though I felt terrified a lot of the time, I would just do it anyway and simply ignore those feelings.

I loved the feeling of the wind in my hair, the sun on my

body and the sensation of freedom, sailing across the water and moving with the wind. There were no thoughts in my head about anything other than windsurfing. I felt so alive.

Everyone in the family had enjoyed themselves so we decided to try the same kind of holiday again the following year. I was always a bit nervous about windsurfing at the start of a holiday because I hadn't tried it for a year, but after a few days it would come back to me and I would spend the next two weeks constantly in the sea, on and off my board, quite happy.

After a few holidays of going windsurfing just once a year, I decided I needed more practice if I was ever to improve significantly, so I joined a windsurfing club in Lochwinnoch, just outside Glasgow. At the first evening social for members, I found that the club consisted mainly of men, but I noticed I didn't feel anxious around them and I started to observe that people who liked windsurfing were happy and positive. And they were keen to help me improve, so my fears, or the memories of my fears, faded like smoke.

About ten years after that first course in Greece, I learned to go into a harness and it really increased the challenge. I needed to reach a certain level of expertise before using a harness, because it enables a surfer to go faster and it requires more skill to control the board. But it meant that my arms stopped feeling like they were being pulled from their sockets, and once I had mastered it, I could relax even more and go faster. It was an exhilarating feeling.

I remember one time when we were on holiday in Turkey;

the wind was barely blowing so I got a lift from the safety boat and they dropped me off far from the beach, where the wind was good. This was something that I wouldn't even have considered doing in the past, but now I loved being out alone in the middle of the sea.

Waiting quietly on my board for the wind, I took in the view of the mountains in the distance, the warm sea beneath me and, overhead, the brilliant blue sky. I felt the warm sun on my face and felt so alive in that moment. Something hit me right then, something profound that marked a real shift in my life and my perception of this life. I realised that all of what I saw was inside me too, that I was looking at nature – and *was* that nature. It's true for all of us and it became so clear in that instant. I couldn't help but feel in awe and think, isn't it all amazing?

I'm still learning how to use my harness, my boards have changed and I can plane (when the board bounces across the water at higher speed) now and again. I have a lot to learn, but I haven't given up. Windsurfing really resonates with my life and reminds me that whatever happens, I will always get back on my board and continue to try and ride the waves. Sometimes I may need help from other people, but a lot of the time I have to do it for myself.

There were times over the years when the safety boats couldn't see me by the rocks or were busy helping capsized boats. Each time, I had to dig deep inside to find my courage and determination to get myself back to the waterfront by pulling myself up onto my board, standing up straight, righting my sail and continuing, no matter what was going on inside me. I couldn't always be rescued.

I was fast learning that while I might experience a lot of anxiety and inadequacy out on my board, I could still find the strength to overcome them and simply keep on sailing.

CHAPTER THIRTY-SIX

KARATE

Shelley, my running friend, asked if I would be interested in going to karate classes with her. Her boys all went and she thought it looked like something we would enjoy since we both loved exercise. The children had been going for a few years and were working their way through their gradings (coloured belts). I thought about it and figured it would be another safe way to put myself in a male-dominated environment, so at the age of forty-one, I found myself going to my first karate class. I wasn't sure what to expect and felt quite nervous, like a new kid at school.

Shelley already knew the *sensei* (martial arts instructor) and he greeted us outside the building when we arrived. He seemed lovely and helped put me at ease, but when we walked into the class, I saw that we were the only women there among about thirty men. I took a deep breath and forged ahead.

The class consisted mainly of black belts and I felt a bit intimidated by them, but I soon discovered that they were all very friendly, welcoming and helpful too. As beginners, we stood at the back of the class while the most experienced stood at the front. One of the black belts gave Shelley and me a private class at the back on stances and basic moves, which we practised most of that night.

The time passed quite quickly and I became totally absorbed in what we were being taught, even though the *sensei* and experienced students made it look a lot easier than it was! Towards the end of the class, a black belt performed a *kata* (choreographed karate moves) for us, and I was totally mesmerised by what I saw.

Everybody sat down and formed a circle around him. He moved beautifully, displaying focus and presence unlike anything I had seen or felt before. The energy he gave out commanded my attention. My friend and I just looked at each other and said, 'Wow!'

We went back every week and soon we decided we liked it enough to invest in a suit. This changed everything for me: I felt very different walking in with a karate suit on because it showed everyone, including Shelley and me, that we were taking it more seriously now.

Although I struggled with lots of elements in the class, I worked well at hiding that. For example, I felt shy and self-conscious when asked to demonstrate something in front of the class. My performance anxiety kicked in and I had to fight with my self-image, pride and feelings of vulnerability to put myself forward – and I did, despite how I felt.

I found it hard to find my voice, especially my *kiai*, which is the shouting noise people use when executing a technique. I heard it constantly all around me in class and I found it very intimidating.

There are many reasons for *kiai*, I learned. It teaches you to breathe out as a way to focus and it aids with the contraction of one's muscles, but more importantly, it's a way to express and declare your energy and fighting spirit, which can be both intimidating to your opponent and self-reassuring at the same time. Try as I might, I couldn't make a sound for many years; I felt too shy and weak.

One night, while the children were being graded, the adult class was held in the gym next door by another *sensei*. He decided it would be fun to try some self-defence moves. One of them was a stranglehold: your opponent had to place their hands around your neck and pretend to be strangling you.

Shelley got over me and put her hands around my neck. In an instant, I was back in that room, with Randall's hands around my neck, banging my head on the floor and screaming at me to be quiet. Shelley must have noticed me struggling and she asked if I was OK. I wasn't, but I said yes all the same and carried on.

As scary as it was for the memories to come up then, I told

myself that these were just pictures in my mind and that it wasn't happening anymore. I forced myself to break away and instead to look at the evidence. Was I back in London? No. Was Randall there with his hands around my neck? No. I was in a class in Glasgow, learning karate: that was the reality.

The *sensei* asked us if we could give him an example of some other kind of hold we'd like to learn to get out of. All I could think of was being thirteen, drunk, on the floor and tied up to the radiator – I knew I didn't have a chance of getting out of that one.

As with windsurfing, I was learning that the more I relaxed with karate, the easier it got and the better I got at it. Surprisingly, karate is a lot about softness and speed rather than power and strength.

In order for me to do well and continue to improve, I had to come out of my head and more into my body. When we learned to punch, I discovered that it started from my heel, through my hips, then out of my arm and into my hand. It was a very different exercise from running. I realised that I could run and not be present or even be in my body at all – I could get lost in my thoughts while running. But this was very different: I had to learn to be present and show up in my body.

A lot of karate requires breathing right from the centre of your gut (*hara*), which in turn affects the energy you give out. Once I dropped more into my gut, without my mind getting involved, the sounds for my *kiai* slowly began to emerge. I realised that it wasn't something that could be taught. Slowly, over time, I found my voice, and it didn't come from the back of my throat but rather from somewhere deep inside me. It felt empowering to use my voice, as if more and more of me was showing up and declaring my existence.

I was getting very used to the men in my class and to being one of the few women there, too. Shelley's boys stopped going to the class and then Shelley too stopped, but I decided to stay because it was helping me in so many ways.

My *sensei* ran two clubs and we would often get visits from some members of the other club, which had a lot of serious competitors in it. One night we were learning a fighting technique from one of the teachers, who was a very successful competitor. He formed a circle and picked people out to fight with him on a one-to-one basis to show us that technique. He asked one of the older women to come and fight him, but she refused… So then he picked me.

Everything in me wanted to say no, but I didn't. I gave it my best, and he could have wiped the floor with me, but didn't. However, I didn't back down and I stood up for myself, trying not to show that I was scared as hell on the inside. This was a breakthrough: I saw that, much as I was doing with windsurfing, I could ignore those internal emotions and carry on if I chose to. So when I chose to do that in this circumstance, it immediately weakened his power over me.

The culture in our *dojo* (class) was one of respect: everyone wanted to see each other improve, and we supported each other in our journeys in whatever ways we could. I was beginning to see men in a very different light.

Not long after I joined, one of the senior black belts developed a brain tumour and, despite many operations and treatments, it became clear he wouldn't survive. Karate was a way of life for him, and I witnessed something so beautiful in his last few months of life that it flipped my views of the men in my class altogether.

The guys in the class would take turns to pick him up and bring him to the class; he was losing his sight now and could no longer drive. They would help him shower afterwards and take him back home. He got weaker and weaker with time and couldn't manage much by the end, but with their help he was there until he moved into a hospice and then passed away.

The love and care from everyone was so beautiful to witness. It really touched my heart, and I knew then that I had nothing to fear from any of those men. In that moment I also knew that in my life, I had seen the best and worst from men.

I didn't really start karate to do my gradings, but my *sensei* encouraged me and he would put me forward to do them whenever he felt I was ready. I knew that a lot of it wasn't about the grading itself; it was more about your attendance and attitude in class, which he was always observing.

For six years I worked away, until one day my grading for first dan (black belt) arrived. I was a nervous wreck, but I passed! It was a great moment, not because I was now a black belt (although that didn't hurt), but because I recognised just how far I had come over the years. I had battled with so many emotions internally and learned to stay with them during my classes, when instinct had told me to run out countless times. Dealing with flashbacks and memories, and carrying on despite them, taught me to stand tall and not be affected by them. I became more grounded, in my body, and confident too. Even though I'm not a great fighter, I'm not afraid to fight – and I found my *kiai*.

CHAPTER THIRTY-SEVEN

WEIGHT TRAINING

As well as filling the roles of best friend, running partner and karate comrade, Shelley was also a Pilates instructor and personal trainer (PT), and she used to train me in the gym once a week. I loved it: we got to spend more time together and she opened up the world of weights to me. She played a pretty major role in my overall emotional wellbeing and physical fitness.

In 2009, the bottom fell out of my world when she told me that she and her family were moving to Israel. The move left a gaping hole in me that has never been filled, and I miss her every day. We spoke and saw each other daily, and connected in a way that didn't need words; we just understood each other.

When I went to the gym by myself, I missed having someone to train me and push me along; it felt lonely. So I decided to find myself a personal trainer to help me reach my goals of getting fitter and stronger. Around this time, a card came through my door from a local PT who was just starting out and offering a great introductory price. He worked at my gym so I decided to call him. I liked what I heard on the phone straight away and decided to have a trial session, even though I was a bit hesitant – I had never trained with a man in the gym.

As soon as I met Patrick, I got a sense he was going to be OK. There was nothing pushy or flashy about him, and I had seen that in lots of other trainers at the gym. He seemed gentle and genuine, was very easy to be around and had my best interests at heart.

He started to teach me all about power lifting, which I loved. It was amazing to see what my body was capable of doing and how it could be pushed. He taught me how to do many lift techniques such as squats, deadlifts and bench presses, as well as Olympic lifting (the clean and jerk and the snatch).

I found that in order to lift heavy things, I had to be really present and in my body because it often required me to dig deep inside and to use all of my energy. As I added more muscle and grew stronger, my body began changing; I started to like it again after so many years of either hating or just ignoring it. My self-esteem improved, too. I was developing focus and determination. As with all the other sports I did, I learned the importance of my breath and that I had to connect with it to help me. Lifting weights and connecting with my breath helped to ground me: I had to be in my body to make it all work.

I started to go into the weights room at my gym, something I had never done before. It was predominantly filled with huge men who sought to lift as much as they could – it looked, smelled and sounded like men. I had always been intimidated by it, felt the overpowering testosterone-ness of it and just plain avoided going in, as did most women I knew. All I could hear was the groaning and straining when the men were lifting and the heavy thuds when they dropped their weights.

At first, I would go in wearing my headphones, avoiding eye contact and just getting on with my session. I got used to seeing the same guys, always in at the same time, and after a while I got a nod or a smile. Gradually, I started to see that they were just like me, wanting to improve their fitness and get stronger, rather than the macho men that I'd first thought they were.

One day I arrived to find I hadn't charged my iPod, which really annoyed me, but I went upstairs to do my session anyway. I walked into the weights room and was setting up to deadlift when one of the guys came over and asked if I could help him with his form. He knew I trained with Patrick, who was very strict on form.

I was quite shocked, in a good way, but said, 'Yes, of course.' He told me that he was impressed by the way I trained and with my discipline. That took me by surprise, but changed something for me, too: I started to see we were all there for the same reason. The men weren't intimidating me or trying to pick me up; we all shared the same passion for weightlifting and improving our technique and strength. I felt respect from them towards me.

After that, I stopped bringing my iPod to the gym. The messages I was putting out, by wearing the earbuds, were 'Keep away' and 'Don't speak to me.' I started to say 'Hi' to everyone when I arrived and they all responded. And if I had a question about lifting, I would ask one of them, no problem. They could see that I knew what I was doing and they started to encourage me, making me feel accepted.

It was another avenue to break down my perceptions of men as well as a lot of other barriers for me. Often I am still the only woman in the weights room, but I don't give it any thought at all and never feel worried about being in an all-male environment. One of the main things I learned in that room was to be more comfortable around men, to look them in the eye and to speak with them completely free of anxiety. My only problem now is that I have to be careful that I don't chat too much and lose focus on my session! This is a problem I like having.

Getting stronger physically has helped not just my body, but my mind, too. Patrick always encouraged me to lift more, and I would say, 'Are you sure? I don't think I can do that!' And then I'd astonish myself when I could – it gave me such a high.

I always felt better after I had trained; I felt the endorphin release, just as I had as a runner, but this was better than the 'runner's high'. I was beginning to see that there was a direct relationship between getting stronger in the gym and getting stronger in my life.

Lifting taught me to step out of my comfort zone and do things I thought I wasn't able to. It taught me to activate my will, showing me that we always have a choice about where we put our focus or energy. It showed me that I was mentally tough – a lot of the lifts are psychological as well. Perhaps I knew I had mental strength, but this showed me the direct translation to physical strength as well. It complemented and reinforced what I was learning in karate.

I used to dread doing front squats – having the bar lean against my throat reminded me of being strangled, which in turn made me panic. But I hid it as much as I could and simply carried on. I decided to do more and more front squats to show myself they were just memories and it wasn't happening again. Lifting, windsurfing and karate all exposed the paper tigers that were my memories.

Knowing that I can deadlift nearly twice my body weight has made me realise that I can achieve much more than I've ever allowed myself to believe, if I put my mind and body to it.

CHAPTER THIRTY-EIGHT

WORKING WITH MEN

While studying for my diploma, I made a decision to leave my job at Women's Aid and get a position in counselling. As much as I loved working with the women who came there for help, I did not love the office politics. It was run as a collective, which meant all eight of us were workers and bosses. I got tired of the battles and power struggles so I took the opportunity to change direction – and on top of that, I loved counselling.

They used to say to us at college that you are sent the clients you need and that each client is a gift. How true that is. There were three clients that worked on me more than I worked on them, and they helped me more than they will ever know.

While I was still in college I had a temporary placement once a week in a doctor's surgery. I was a bit anxious, but I was keen to see 'real' people since we had only practised on each other in college. Despite all that practice, nothing prepared me for my first ever client.

He was a huge guy, about six feet tall, seemingly the same dimension across, and his presence filled the entire room. He was Italian and would sit hands on thighs with his legs spread wide open, always leaning towards me. I felt nervous to be alone with him in the room, but told myself this was normal since I had primarily worked with women and the few men who were on my course. But no matter what I told myself, my nerves started to take over and I couldn't focus on what he was saying during the session. I felt a wave of panic rise up as he sat semi-blocking the door, and I worried about how I would get out if he tried anything on with me. Ironically, I told myself that this was crazy; I needed to find a way to put my fears to one side and be there for my client. But I didn't know how.

Towards the end of the session, he told me the reason he had been suspended from work: he was caught using the Internet. He said he was just looking at pictures of children but his work described it as child pornography. Oh, God! This just panicked me even more, so I quickly ended the session.

I went back to college and took it to a supervision session, where Ron gave me ways to ground myself before I went in so that I could be present and available for the client. But I couldn't do it and panicked even more; my mind filled with judgements about the man sitting in front of me and I just wanted to get out. So I decided to tell him that he was only entitled to have three sessions, rather than the eight that he should have been given, since the waiting list was so long and time was so short.

After his last session the following week I felt so guilty; I hadn't given him a chance at all, I was so preoccupied with my process and what was going on inside my mind. This couldn't go on if I wanted to be a good counsellor, seeing both men and women.

I was appalled at my behaviour and decided that because I felt so uncomfortable working with men, I would get as many male clients as I could to try and get past this. So as soon as I saw a man's name on the waiting list, I would put my name next to it. In essence, I was leaning into the wind.

My next male client had anger issues, and in time went on to reveal that a stranger had raped him when he was thirteen and on holiday with his parents. He really wanted to work through this and felt it was the root of his anger. Recently he'd had dreams about the assault in great detail, he told me. I was really touched by what he said.

Together we explored what had happened and I could see the impact it was having on him. When I got him to connect more to himself, I was so familiar with all of his reactions. He told me that he had felt dirty for all these years (he was in his thirties now) and had bleached his body daily; it was his fault, he felt, because his mum had told him not to go where he did. He had so much shame that he could hardly look at me.

I knew that what had helped me most, regardless of the

emotional difficulty, was to connect to the pain, to stay with the facts of the event, so I did my best to guide him through that. I encouraged him to make eye contact with me, while focusing on his breath, to start the internal connection to himself.

He felt sick in the sessions as his body started to release the memories that he had blocked up and stored deep within himself; he would shake violently from head to toe. His tears began to flow and flow in each session, grieving for his younger self. I just encouraged and supported him as best I could on this painful journey.

But I couldn't believe what I was watching; I was so moved to see a man in front of me open up in the vulnerable way he did – I felt his fear. His courage touched me and changed me, too. Working with him over several months showed me how similar men are to women. I had separated them in my mind, but I saw how their emotions, feelings and responses were just like women's.

It moved me so much to see a man cry in the way he did, that often my eyes filled up too. I suddenly saw this man as another human being who had been hurt and was no different to me or anyone else. From that moment on, my opinion of men was altered and I saw them as my equals rather than enemies or people to be feared.

After that, it was much easier for me to work with men. I was so much more relaxed and didn't need to be the one sitting nearer to the door. More importantly, though, I was able to be present in the sessions without fears or vivid memories intruding on the work. Finally, I could hear and work with whatever a client would bring to a session.

Another male client I met showed me exactly how much I had moved on from my fears. He was a returning client of mine who originally came to me with grief over the cot death of his young son, which resulted in the break-up of his relationship. We had connected well and established a good working relationship. He processed his grief well: it was very painful for him, but he slowly came to terms with the loss of his child.

So I was surprised to hear that he wanted to come back. In the first session, he revealed to me that he hadn't been honest the last time we had met; he was in fact a convicted sex offender and had served time in prison for raping another man. I was shocked and totally surprised by his confession, but I also recognised the risk he took in telling me, because another centre had asked him to leave when they found out about his conviction.

I couldn't turn my back on him now and reject him, too. Besides, I had worked with and respected him as another human being in our previous sessions so how could I undo that? This man evoked no fear in me at all and I continued to work with him for many months.

He showed me that while this may have been one side to him, it was not all of him, just as I wasn't simply a woman who had been raped. I saw that he didn't come into the world as a rapist, and when the facts unfolded, it turned out he was very much a victim as well, having also been raped when he was young.

He was struggling so much with what he'd done to another person, and I felt that from him. I could not help but be moved, and any judgements I'd formed about him when he told me about his conviction completely evaporated. Had it been a few years before, and I'd been told he was a convicted rapist, I would have at least refused to work with him and probably not even wanted to look at him. Because of him, I have tried hard to never again judge anyone else I come across, client or otherwise. I have no idea what is going on for them and what led them to where they are in the journey of their life.

My client unknowingly helped me to drop any revenge and hatred I had towards the boys that had raped me, too. I saw the humanity not just in him, but in them as well.

CHAPTER THIRTY-NINE

REVELATION

I had heard that some people from Emahó's workshops had taken a cactus juice called San Pedro for therapeutic reasons. From talking to some of the people who had done it, my interest became piqued. Rainer, one of the men who worked in Emahó's crew, came to Scotland twice a year to run four-day workshops that included drinking San Pedro every day – I signed right up.

I learned that the juice is extracted from the San Pedro cactus, and that for hundreds of years it has been used by shamans and healers in Peru, but that was about all I knew. It appealed to me because I felt the need for a breakthrough. Therapy was going well; I could see I was making progress and doors were opening up inside me. I wanted to keep that momentum going and I thought perhaps San Pedro could help.

There were about fifteen of us who took over a hostel in Glenfeshie, one of the most beautiful parts of Scotland I have ever seen. It was early spring 2013 and an unusually clear and temperate weekend, especially for Scotland. We started all four days the same way: with a small, light breakfast, followed by drinking the San Pedro juice at eleven o'clock. It was certainly an unusual way to start the day!

And it was the foulest thing I had ever drunk. The texture was thick and lumpy; the taste beyond bitter – I gagged after each gulp. Fortunately, I didn't have to drink much and it didn't take long for me to feel the effects, maybe fifteen minutes. It took about twenty minutes before I wanted to get out of the house and be outdoors, away from people. There was a river nearby and I headed in that direction. Within moments of walking, I started to feel pains over my body, especially my stomach, where I felt like I was being kicked.

Sometimes the sensation of getting kicked was strong enough to take my breath away; my ribs felt so sore. While that was going on, I also saw images of being kicked and punched from that night, over and over again. My God, I was so fed up with seeing those details again. Would I ever drain the swamp? I wondered. Outwardly, I felt I had come so far, overcoming so many fears, but this was showing me that the trauma was still lingering inside me, even if it was on an unconscious level.

I soon discovered that the plant was stripping me bare of the everyday habits, thoughts and actions that defined 'Madeleine'. My daily life was like a merry-go-round that I had just stepped off, I could clearly see. Our days are so busy, so demanding of our attention, that we rarely have time to truly slow down enough to see a different perspective. This plant did exactly that; it was as though the veils of the Madeleine who lived in society had been lifted, leaving me with what was inside, beyond the roles I've played (daughter, sister, wife, mother, friend, employee, etc.) all my life. I felt a kind of liberation, but the effects of the plant were strong and, as the day went on, I found myself getting more and more emotionally distressed.

I watched the other participants having a great and joyful time, climbing trees, swimming in the river and laughing with each other. But I couldn't join in with them; what I felt was not joyous and the physical pain in my stomach continued to distress me.

My body started to distort into its old holding patterns from that night and I was shocked. Hadn't I cleaned all that up? But my hands turned into fists and my legs kicked the ground as if I was trying to get away from someone. No, I had *not* cleaned all that up.

Every now and again, Rainer would come and find each of us to check that we were OK, but every time he came near me and tried to console me in some way, I pushed him away. The urge to fight with him was almost too strong for me to hold back. He asked if he was too close and I said yes, so he stayed away.

When it got too cold, I decided to go back to the house to warm up. On the way there, I passed through a field of broken and dead trees. Rather than seeing it for what it literally was, I saw the field as a graveyard, filled with broken limbs and dead bodies. I sat down on a tree trunk to take in the picture and started to cry.

To me, it was a vivid reflection of what we as humans do to each other, how we hurt each other over and over again. It brought up all my old questions: what is the point of violence? Why do we do what we do to each other? What will break the chain? In that moment there was a shift inside me. I was no longer upset about what had happened to me, but for all the women across the planet who had been raped and killed: it's not just me, it's us.

I saw Rainer in the distance walking towards me, and when he got closer, he could see I was crying. 'Look at what we do. We hurt, break and kill each other!' I said. At this he pointed to the mountains filling the sky to the west, and I was moved by their rugged beauty. He just replied, 'It's both.'

I realised it was one of the great paradoxes of life, that there is good and bad going on, simultaneously, all the time. It was clear that I had to learn to find a way to hold both at the same time and be OK with it.

I had thought that I would find a place in the house where I could get warm and be by myself, but I heard music playing and couldn't resist its pull. It really got inside me. Then Rainer started playing the didgeridoo and it instantly triggered something in my body; I began shaking and crying.

My God, more of this?

I was so frustrated; I saw the same images of what was done to me. When would it all stop? I asked myself.

I did the course four more times and with each one I got a bit more trusting towards the people there – and Rainer too. Whenever I had a flashback, he would approach and ask if it was OK to sit with me. I didn't feel threatened anymore. He would hold my hand, I would feel the vibrations of fear swell and rise up in me and the tears would stream from my eyes. Over time, it didn't feel like trauma anymore, but a great sadness and grief for my lost childhood.

The last time I took San Pedro, I told myself that I wanted to see the worst that was done to me. Tired of being affected by it, I wanted to test myself. I felt brave. The memories came like a river breaking through a dam. With every image and memory, I could feel my body wanting to react as it always had, but this time was different. I refused to allow it; I stayed steady, watching the show with no reaction.

This was the shift I'd been seeking. I learned that I had a choice – to go back into my trauma or to not allow myself to be seduced by it any longer. Yes, seduced. It was the first time I'd seen it that way. My mind would show me memories and I would react – that was the way it worked. Well, not any more. This was one of the daily veils that had clouded my life, and by understanding this dynamic I was throwing off the veil: it could no longer keep me trapped, conditioned, suppressed. It felt amazing not to be affected by all that I was seeing and remembering – a liberation I hadn't ever imagined before. I found myself feeling light, joyful and playful, just like those people at the workshop I had watched years ago, laughing and enjoying each other. Now I could join them.

I could see the power of choice that we humans have as never before – and I chose not to be affected by it anymore. It felt so clean inside me, a feeling I'd not known since I was a young girl. It gave me belief in myself and hope not just for me but for all girls and women who survive violence. Then it hit me: this was the final act of my best revenge.

CHAPTER FORTY

INK

I was feeling so different now; my mind was completely calm and I hardly ever thought about what happened to me so many years before. When my mind did go there, none of the hooks caught me and pulled me into the patterns I'd been caught in for most of my life. All my fears and phobias had vanished; it was liberation beyond description.

Simple things used to be big issues for me, but now, for example, I could walk into a dark room in my home without putting the light on straight away. I confidently (and noisily) moved the wheelie bins out to the end of the garden any time of day or night. Now I looked forward to meeting people rather than fearing them. Travel was no longer a source of stress and anxiety, just excitement. Nothing seemed to trigger any reaction like it would have done in the past.

The stress that shaped my every thought and movement had vanished. Sleep came more easily and the nightmares had ceased. I had a greater appreciation of life and saw goodness in everything. I realised how lucky I was to be alive; I felt happy. Most of my attention used to be fixed on my own personal safety, and now I focused on loving and living my life. My intimate relationships grew warmer and stronger. I even felt a closeness, or at least an openness, to the people I would meet during the course of my day.

I had no idea how tense I had been at home until this new softness came in and exposed the contrast; all the little things that had bothered me before no longer pushed my buttons. Can one person's moods really affect a house that much? Um, yeah! The more I relaxed, the more everyone in the house did, too. I saw a beautiful ripple effect. My previous need to be in control meant everything used to have to be neat and tidy and in its place, as if proper placement could mask what had happened. Messes became easy to handle – and lasted a bit longer!

It had taken me all those years, all this work, to feel truly alive without any thoughts of the past holding me back. It took me all this time to really understand that the trauma wasn't happening anymore, and if it seemed like it was happening, I knew it was only in my mind, only my memories, playing old movies in my head. I felt profound understanding; I felt freed from my past.

I hardly recognised the person I used to be. Strangely, that's what the thirteen-year-old girl thought about herself after she'd been raped: she hardly recognised the person she used to be. Now it had come full circle and I had more connection with both of those girls, from before and after.

Now I could say the word 'rape' without recoiling, if only internally. I could look back over what was done and just accept it. I'd never felt like this before and I absolutely loved it. There seemed to be more space inside me and more of me was showing up. And that was when I knew that whatever had been done to me, nothing could ever hurt the real essence of me; that would always be in there, it was just a matter of finding it again. They had hurt my body, but I'm not my body. They traumatised my mind, but I'm not my mind; I am much more than that.

Over and over, I thought back to the young man I had run my marathon with, all those years ago; the one who was covered in tattoos. Every one of them told a story from his life – and now I wanted to do something to mark this turning point in my own life.

After looking at loads of photos and meanings of tattoos on the Internet, I came across these words by Doe Zantamata, from a Facebook page called 'Happiness in Your Life' about metamorphosis and personal transformation, which resonated so much with me:

On the journey between caterpillar and butterfly, the caterpillar encloses itself into a cocoon. Within that cocoon, the entire caterpillar is broken down into a soup-like mixture. Just about all of the major structures are broken down and rebuilt, including the heart. Soon, the butterfly emerges. Hardly a trace of the caterpillar remains. The butterfly feels free to fly. Personal transformation is much the same. Tired of just eating, working, existing, we go within and close off somewhat from the outside world. We re-examine all of our beliefs: what we were told, what we learned. The process takes much longer than a few days, but sooner or later, we rebuild. We replace false beliefs, held in our minds, with truth held in our hearts. We shed the old, and begin to emerge anew. Released from our limitations and negative beliefs, we become free to fly.

I felt they described my journey so well; my head and heart were so contrastingly different to those of my thirteen-year-old self – I had to have a butterfly.

I decided that I wanted a man to do the tattoo for me – it seemed important, more proof that I was OK so I researched tattoo artists and came across Frank McNab from Creative Art Tattoo Studio in Glasgow. I joined his Facebook page and just watched his posts for a while to see not just what he would post, but also the tone and feel of what he posted. It had to be good, because I felt that part of who he was would go into me, into that tattoo.

I quickly saw that he had an amazing attitude towards life, sending positive messages out every day. Despite what one might think of a man covered in tattoos, he loved his cats, meditated, did yoga and enjoyed his garden. From how he looked, I would have steered clear of him in the past, but I had learned not to judge anyone by how they looked and I really liked what I saw and felt from his page.

Just before my forty-seventh birthday, I made the appointment, paid my deposit and sent Frank an image of the tattoo I wanted. I felt a bit nervous going in, but was quickly reassured by his warm and easy demeanour. We chatted about the size and placement, deciding on my left shoulder. I was a bit concerned about the pain, but it wasn't bad at all. He was a genuine guy with a lovely smile and I discovered he loved the gym, too. So we chatted away about that, and I never felt worried that a man wasn't just seeing my body, but tattooing it as well.

As I left, he said, 'Welcome to your new addiction,' and I said no, no, it was just this one time. He replied, 'You'll be back!' And he was right: one would not do it!

I continued reading about tattoos and their meanings, and kept coming across images of the lotus flower. A very determined flower that grows out of the marsh and swamps to finally open its bloom at the water's surface, it represents awareness rising out of chaos and a new beginning; it sounded like me. It's used a lot in Tibetan tattoos and reminded me of my monk.

When my memories of that night returned, it was only when I fully accepted the monk was there that I finally accepted everything they did to me. When I dismissed him in my mind, I also dismissed what was done. So I had to accept all that took place that night, which included the monk, to finally face it and be OK with it. The more I argued about his presence, the more I kept myself stuck. As I look back on it now, I don't think I would have survived had he not been there, protecting me. So I wanted to remind myself how protected I had been that night and how I had emerged from the mud like the lotus, opening up and connecting with my life.

So, in keeping with Frank's prediction, I made another appointment about six months later. He laughed when I walked back into his studio. This tattoo would be located on my right thigh. In my mind, it was roughly where the monk had been sitting next to me that night.

I had also read that the lotus is often a symbol of a story that is waiting to be told. Over the two hours that the tattoo took to complete, I told Frank some of my story. He was moved and expressed his anger at men who treat women like that, which touched me. Again, I felt totally relaxed and didn't panic at all despite the fact that my legs were exposed to him.

My last tattoo was a surprise present from my children for my fiftieth birthday. I tried to guess for weeks what my gift could be, but they remained silent and revelled in their secret. Everything I guessed came back with a resounding 'No!' until I actually guessed on the day and asked, 'Are we going to see Frank?'

Anna said yes, and handed me a card. Inside I found these words: '*Just a small reminder to let you know we love you! If it wasn't for you being brave and not letting what happened to you take over your life, we wouldn't be here. Thank you for showing us that positive things can come out of <u>any</u> situation. Every time you look at this, it's a reminder – that's what you should think of*. She had drawn three little hearts called Anna, Mimi and Leila, and told me I could decide where they would go.

I was so moved; my eyes filled up with tears. Reading those words meant so many different things to me. Apart from the obvious ones, that they loved me and were proud of my achievements, it also meant that they appreciated their lives, too, and I had shown them that it's never what happens to you that is important, but what you do with what happens to you – it's what my parents showed me.

CHAPTER FORTY-ONE

GIVING
IT OXYGEN

I had been attending Emahó's seminars for about five years and had spoken to him many times about what had happened to me. Often it was about whether I could trust the memories that were bubbling up and, every time, he would reassure me, echoing what Ron had told me: the memories are real and I wouldn't make them up. It took me that much time not only to muster the desire and courage to look at the memories, but also to accept that I could completely shut out such extreme events and keep them from my conscious mind for so long. Our coping mechanisms are complex and geared towards keeping us going, living our lives as best we can.

Emahó said that since all of the memories had returned, it would be really good for me to write down a detailed account of what happened that night and give it to him. I said I didn't think I could do that; I was too ashamed for him to read what they'd done. It was one thing to remember it all and be OK with it, another for others to know what had happened. Only Steven and Ron knew everything that had been done to me, could I expose myself that much to another person? And if so, to what benefit?

Over the next four years I would think about what Emahó had suggested and I would try and start it, but would end up putting it away, stopping far short of really getting it out. Countless times I started and stalled, until one night in Basel in April 2014, while I was attending one of Emahó's workshops, when something kick-started inside me.

I picked up my iPad and started to write... and write. It felt as if my hands were automatic, writing by themselves. I sat up until the night sky gave way to daylight, the words flowing effortlessly from my fingertips for hours on end.

And yet, paradoxically, as easily as the words poured forth, reliving the story, in full detail, all at once, felt emotionally taxing. All the shame, guilt and sadness came flooding back, at times overwhelming and stopping me in my tracks. Unearthing those memories caused so many feelings, which I thought I had resolved, to bubble up to the surface. However, the process was nothing short of cathartic. Looking down at the twelve pages, written out in a stream of consciousness, it didn't feel like me anymore: that naïve young girl who was just looking for a fun night out with boys was long gone. And I couldn't wrap my head around the violence that two young men could do to another human being. There was no escaping the facts when I saw them written down in black and white; my heart couldn't deny it any longer. It happened, it all happened.

I went to the workshop that day exhausted, more from the process of writing and remembering than from any lack of sleep.

When I cried at the end of every dance, I would always feel embarrassed; the room would be churchly quiet except for the music playing – and my sobbing. As hard as I tried, I couldn't stop it. Most people were used to it, but that day a woman asked me, and not in a kindly manner, to leave. Initially, I said no, but then everything just welled up inside me and I ran from the room.

After some time, I returned to the room and approached Emahó. I told him what she'd said and that I feared she was simply the voice for everyone in the room, who was also annoyed with me and wanted me to stop crying. He explained that she was just young and that my tears disturbed her – and that was a door for her. My tears were good for people because by disturbing them, it gave them an opportunity to drop into their hearts, he told me.

Over the years I had come to understand that when people were affected by my tears and came over to me for whatever reason, something had stirred inside them, some kind of chord had been struck, but they couldn't stay with it. It was easier to come and support me rather than go within to look at what was going on in their own lives.

Before saying goodbye, I told him that I had written out the events of that night. He asked me to send it to him.

A few weeks later he called me and told me that he wanted to speak about what had happened to me at his next workshop. I expressed my hesitance, but he said it would really help other people. My God, it was hard enough to pass that along to Emahó! I felt so nervous, unsure, and worried that people's opinions of me would change; I wondered if they would believe me.

He said he wanted to educate people on what can take place on this planet and what we, as human beings, are capable of doing to each other. People grow up in a kind of protected bubble, he told me, and he wanted to use my story to wake them up to this. Most people never encounter real violence, they simply read about it or hear stories about it – it keeps the violence abstract, as if it doesn't really exist. When they hear about what happened to me, someone they know, it will drive the reality home. Emahó had been my teacher now for nearly nine years and I trusted him, so I said yes.

I told him that he could speak about me on condition that he call me afterwards to let me know how it went, and that I receive a recording of his speech so I could hear exactly what was said. Agreed. So at one of the busiest workshops, in Teufen, Switzerland, Emahó shared my story with several hundred people.

Afterwards, Emahó called and told me it had gone really well. For years he had been waiting for me to write my story so that he could share it with people: he wanted them to know that some people go through very difficult things, but that we can deal with them with no hate or revenge. He said we tend to focus our attention on the beautiful things in life and not on the other side. I asked if he had let people read what I had written and he confirmed he had.

I was mortified that all these people had read about the most intimate experience of my life. He had asked me to include all of the details, names and places, and I hadn't left anything out. There was so much shame rising up and spilling out of me that it shook me to the core; I felt sick.

I was embarrassed about them knowing all the details of the rape and torture, but more upset that they would now know about my monk. To me that was even more personal than all the other details. I wondered how I could ever walk back into the room again and face them all: the most private aspects of my life were now public domain.

When I listened to the recording from that day, I discovered that he hadn't held back when describing what had been done to me. Hearing him describe the details of the assault out loud chilled me to the bone. My physical frame shook from a place deep inside me and tears flowed for my younger self.

During the next few weeks I listened to the teaching over and over again. Something seemed to open inside me, more and more with each listen, as my shame and guilt rose up and then dropped away.

In May 2014, I attended the workshop in Cork, Ireland

– my first since the teaching about the rape. Walking into that room was so hard: I had no idea who had heard the teaching (it hadn't been made public on Emahó's website, as teachings usually were), or who had read my story. I felt so vulnerable and exposed to them all, as if I had walked into the room naked.

Unbeknown to me, Emahó had asked my fellow students not to question me about my story. I could feel everyone's curious gazes and minds upon me. Resisting my immediate urge to escape, I resolved to stay as grounded and as steady as I could. I had been utterly disarmed through my vulnerability, but in that moment I realised that since I had nothing to be ashamed of, there was no reason to feel uncomfortable. My concerns evaporated on the spot.

I really wanted to get feedback from people, to find out what effect, if any, the story had had on them. So I started by sitting with a man that I knew well from Glasgow. I had to start gently! He told me he was deeply moved by what he'd heard and that he felt fortunate to know me. As a child he had been beaten by his mother to within inches of his life. He'd been addicted to drugs, served time in prison and by all means had a very rough life. But he, too, had found a way to turn it around: he could relate to my story in a very personal sense and it had showed him that many people face terrible adversity and fight back. He was not alone.

The next workshop was in my home town of Glasgow and, again, I could feel people's eyes on me as I came in the door.

That was no problem at all. Again I sought feedback and was once more amazed by their replies.

Some women had also been raped, and hearing my story had made them examine their own. It made me wonder how many women we know have been raped, but tell no one or very few people. One man told me about how he had held onto a grudge against a former business partner who had swindled him, but on hearing what I was able to forgive, he found himself letting go of it. The more I opened up to people and gave them the signal it was OK to talk to me about it, the more they approached me with incredible openness and candour. I was seeing exactly what Emahó meant when he'd said that going public would help not just me, but other people, too.

I asked a few close friends for their responses and was simultaneously touched and astounded by their reactions: they talked of my bravery and courage and questioned whether they themselves could have walked it out just as I had. But they also spoke of using parts of my story to help them move on from issues that they'd held on to for many years.

I saw in that moment the healing power of my story, and I knew with complete certainty that it was the right decision to share it, to give it oxygen. Different people identified with different elements of my experience and it touched both men and women alike. But what seemed to strike the deepest chord with most people was not just my ability to heal and rebuild my life, but the fact that I was able to truly forgive my rapists.

CHAPTER FORTY-TWO

GOING PUBLIC

During the time I was in therapy with Ron, I thought a lot about forgiveness. One day, while surfing the Internet, I came across an organisation called The Forgiveness Project. I wondered if they could help me explore a different way of thinking towards the young men who raped me. Intrigued by their website, I dug deeper to find out more about their mission and approach to forgiveness.

I learned that the founder, Marina Cantacuzino, had been collecting and sharing stories since 2004 from people who were both survivors and perpetrators of violence and crime, with the intent of helping all parties to move forward in productive ways beyond resentment, revenge or hatred. Her goal was to promote reconciliation and forgiveness. Reading the stories posted on the website, I was touched by the journeys people had taken, and how they had transformed their lives and moved forward through forgiveness; I also understood their struggles all too well. I acknowledged that at times my thoughts had been, in essence, no different from those of the young men who raped me. I carried strong, revengeful thoughts, wishing they would be kidnapped, tied up and raped, just as they had done to me. In time, I understood that such thoughts made me no different from them, but I've always believed that something good can come out of something bad, and all of the stories on the website echoed that feeling.

It was after Emahó had delivered his teaching about me in Teufen that I found myself on the organisation's Facebook page, commenting on a post about rape. Through that post, I made contact with a woman called Rosalyn Boyce and we connected straight away. We started to message each other privately, away from the public page, and I not only felt an instant kinship with her, but was also very moved by her story.

Sixteen years ago, Rosalyn had been raped by a serial rapist in her home while her two-year-old daughter lay sleeping and her husband was in hospital. So much of what we shared together resonated with me and I just felt she understood me completely. We communicated in a way that made words seem, at times, unnecessary.

I was amazed by her strength and resilience. She had spent many years speaking in prisons, telling her story to prisoners as part of the restorative justice work of The Forgiveness Project. Not only this, but she would also soon be having a face-to-face meeting, in prison, with the man who had raped her. Her bravery was fierce and it touched me deeply.

All the while I was getting braver, sharing some details of my story on The Forgiveness Project's page. Marina Cantacuzino told me that my comments had been helpful to those using the page. In turn I told her how interested I was in the project and asked if there was anything I could do to get involved. I explained how, for me, forgiveness had been the only way forward, and that it had changed my life immensely when I embraced it. Marina asked me to tell her a bit more, so I emailed her the twelve pages I had written for Emahó.

She told me that my story had been deeply upsetting to read, but that it was also extraordinary how I had come through it all – it reminded her of Rosalyn's story. She went on to tell me that she would like to include it as one of the stories on the website and asked if that would be OK with me. My thoughts went to Rosalyn, how she was planning to meet the man who had raped her, and I thought to myself, if she could do that, then I could share my story, too.

Marina said it could just go up on the website, not the Facebook page, that it need not include a photo and that I could remain anonymous, if I chose to. She knew that most of my friends and family didn't have much or any knowledge of what I had experienced. I decided that I didn't have anything to hide anymore; I had held on to inappropriate shame for too long and it was time to stop hiding. My name and photo went right there on the page.

Years before, in 2008, I had shared my story in an Edinburgh-based newspaper as part of a Rape Crisis campaign called 'This is not an excuse to rape me.' But I only used my first name, and there was no photo. I still felt too shy, too ashamed, too concerned of other people's opinions, and that held me back. This time I had to do this, not just for me, but for others, too. Marina and I edited the piece considerably, leaving out a lot of the detail. I talked it over with Steven and he was, as always, completely supportive. I knew this would be a far cry from sharing it with a few hundred people at a workshop; it would reach a much wider audience, far beyond my control.

I wanted to give my family a chance to read my story first, before it went public, so I sent them all an email, explaining my intentions and asking if they wanted to read it first. I was a bit nervous taking this first step, but I only received love and support back from them. Marina emailed over the final copy, I approved it and it went live on the Forgiveness Project website on 22 September 2014.

In order to drive more people to the site, I decided to share the post on Facebook and included this message: 'Not sure if many of you know my story from when I was younger, but I have decided to go public about being raped. It has affected me in different ways for some time, but I have worked with it for many years and I'm really OK now, which is why I can do this. I know that I carried guilt and shame for many years, which didn't belong to me, and I want to let other women know this and that they can get past it too, if they choose to.

In some ways it has shaped my life and made me who I am, but I'm also so much more than one night! Thank you xx.' Then I clicked the 'share' button and posted it.

I completely underestimated the effect it would have. Within moments of it going live, messages of support started to pour in. A lot of friends were shocked that I had kept it from them, and even those who did know about the rape were surprised because they'd had no idea how violent it was. I received many text messages, phone calls, visits, flowers, cards and letters from so many friends; it touched me so much. And people started to share the link on Facebook, over and over again, reaching out more every time. It helped me to stand even straighter in my life, to be accepted with no judgement and to be believed. But what convinced me more than anything else that I had made the right decision to share my story were the many messages I received from women, who reached out to me to tell me their own stories of sexual abuse and rape. Within a few weeks, over twenty women had shared their stories with me, including two who disclosed to me things they had never told anyone else before. After a month, I had lost count of the women who had reached out to me. I heard from women I knew and women I'd never met, both living in the UK and abroad.

I was beginning to understand why Marina called us 'story healers' and not 'storytellers'. Many told me that they admired my courage and bravery for sharing, but more importantly, that my strength had given them hope that they could get past what had happened to them, even if they weren't ready to talk about it yet.

Women I knew would come up to me in the street or at the supermarket and tell me it had happened to them, too. At first I felt a bit awkward seeing people face-to-face once I had gone public, but again, I received so much support that it confirmed I had done the right thing. Many men reached out to me too, with messages of support or in person. That was something I didn't expect and I found it so moving. They told me how I'd helped them to understand a bit more about what a woman can go through, both during and after rape, and the serious effects it can have.

I was beginning to see that different parts of my story had resonated with people in different ways, and that their comments came from where their issues were or where they were stuck. Some were upset that I had been in hospital, others identified with my struggle to become a mother and many were touched by the love between Steven and me.

I knew it had been a big step for me, but all of this reassured me it had been the right one. I'd hoped my story would help other people, and already I was feeling the goodness and healing coming from it. By sharing it, I wanted to break the silence, not just for me but for others too. The simple act of sharing, of telling one's story, can do so much. It was beginning to feel like I had a duty, now that I was at peace with it all, to do all I could. I became even more determined to be the voice for others who couldn't yet find theirs, because I discovered that their stories were mine, too.

CHAPTER FORTY-THREE

MEETING MARIAN

I discovered that The Forgiveness Project also held public talks, which they referred to as conversations, featuring the actual storytellers themselves. They are conducted as a way to help create awareness and education, using real stories to encourage the audience to not only consider different options (other than hate and revenge), but also to see, with their own eyes, what's possible.

Unfortunately for me, most of the conversations took place in London, and that was not an easy trek to make during the week for a working wife and mum from Glasgow. However, I noticed that there was one scheduled in Edinburgh in a few months' time, so I contacted Marina Cantacuzino to get a ticket and to arrange a meeting with her after the event; we hadn't actually met in person yet.

She told me that Marian Partington, a storyteller, was due to be speaking at a school in Glasgow the next month. Perfect! The school was about five minutes away from my house, and I couldn't wait to meet Marian and hear her story. Marina told me that this wasn't a public event; Marian would be speaking to school pupils during the day and then to an invited audience, mainly from multi-faith groups, in the evening. But I managed to get a ticket from the organiser, and I let Marian know I would be there.

I felt a bit nervous but mainly excited to meet someone from the organisation. When I gave my name at the door, I saw that they had written 'The Forgiveness Project' alongside my name as the organisation I was with. That gave me an unexpected sense of pride and belonging.

One of the pupils from the school escorted me upstairs and chatted with me along the way. She asked me what I did for the organisation, and I explained that my story had just gone up on its website recently. Then she asked me my name and stopped right in her tracks when I told her. She looked at me and told me she was studying forgiveness in her modern studies class; she had read my story and hadn't stopped thinking about it since. She revealed that she felt lucky because she had put herself in a very similar situation when she was younger, but that nothing had happened to her. I felt amazed that this young woman was able to open up to me only because she had read my story; I couldn't imagine that it would have happened otherwise.

I went into the hall, picked up a glass of juice and went to look at the exhibition on display. Called 'The F Word', it had been created from a collection of stories and photos from the Forgiveness Project website. I knew it had been taken around the world and I wanted to see it for myself; I found it powerful and thought-provoking.

As I walked around the exhibition, I met a teacher that I knew from my children's primary school. She told me she had recently read my story on the website and that it had affected her, too. She went on to tell me of her surprise: she would never have suspected what I had been through, given the way I am. It was a genuine and touching compliment.

I recognised Marian from her photo and went over to introduce myself to her. She greeted me with a lovely, warm hug. She was on a tight schedule and had to keep moving so we arranged to meet up at the end of the evening.

We were called to take our seats and, after some introductions, Marian started to speak. I knew that her sister was Lucy Partington, who had been abducted and murdered by Fred and Rosemary West in the early 1970s, but it was very different to hear the story being spoken out loud. The whole room was mesmerised by her. I understood intimately all the different stages she had been through on her journey and identified with them all, too: fear, grief, denial, rage and, eventually, peace with forgiveness. She saw that she could either sink into the depths of despair and remain closed-off to the world or face what had happened to Lucy with an open heart; she understood that she had a choice.

Marian talked about the work she did as a storyteller in schools and prisons, and the impact that the story had on the people who listened to it, giving them a chance to find their humanity for themselves. She had written to Rosemary West in prison, saying she recognised that Rosemary was a victim, too (Rosemary had been sexually abused by her father and brother; she was also abducted and raped at the age of fifteen. Her father continued to rape her as an adult and even raped one of her daughters). Rosemary never responded to her letters. She also spoke of making contact with one of their daughters, herself a victim of sexual abuse at the hands of Fred and Rosemary, and how she'd written to Fred's brother, who had replied, saying he hoped something good could come out of all of this. Finally, she ended her talk with a Chinese saying that has stayed with me: 'He who does not forgive digs two graves.'

The attendees were invited to break up into smaller groups to answer questions that had been prepared by The Forgiveness Project to promote discussion and further understanding. I recognised one of the women in my group from my synagogue. She asked who I was here with and I told her that I was one of the stories from the Forgiveness Project website. Everyone in my small group encouraged me to tell them my story, and when I did, I witnessed a range of emotions from them. Some were angered, others weren't sure they could have forgiven in the way I had, but all were touched by my journey. The woman I knew told the group that I had a beautiful family and that she, just like the teacher from my children's school, would never have guessed what was hidden behind my smiles.

I didn't think my journey was so extraordinary, but the more I opened up to people, the more evidence I received to show me that it was. I knew that a lot of people could get stuck, getting caught in their rage and hate, but I hadn't. I was learning that my determination to be identified as more than a victim of rape and to make my best revenge plan a reality had worked better than I had allowed myself to see.

Marian's compassion and understanding shone through as she spoke that night, and I was amazed by how she could speak so calmly and eloquently about it all. But it also encouraged and motivated me to find my voice as well, and I made a decision while she spoke that I would use my story to motivate and inspire people in much the same way. Sharing my story wasn't about helping me anymore, it was about helping others. I realised, too, why I loved being part of this organisation: all of our journeys had led us to drop into our hearts and embrace a greater understanding and compassion for the human predicament. We are all born innocent, but with time we are exposed to so many environmental conditions that shape and influence us, such as our parents, friends, schoolmates, gangs, films, music, television and countless other sources of violence and abuse in our societies. For too many people, constant exposure to violence will lead them to believe it's an acceptable form of action.

At the end of the evening, I went up to speak to Marian

again and told her how much her story resonated with me. I shared with her that I could so easily have been murdered that night, just like her sister Lucy, and was so grateful that I hadn't been. It was like sitting with an old friend, and I wished I could have spent more time with her. There was so much peace and calmness emanating from her that it was hard not to be moved by her presence.

We said goodbye, hugged again and I asked her to sign my copy of her book, *If You Sit Very Still*. She simply wrote, 'Now you must speak.'

CHAPTER FORTY-FOUR

ENDINGS AND BEGINNINGS

I started to connect more and more with people from The Forgiveness Project and with like-minded people through social media. I was so comforted to discover that there were so many people out there doing their bit for peace and embracing an alternative way, rather than holding on to revenge and hate.

I met people who were victims of crime, like me, and perpetrators, all of whom had turned things around and made positive changes in their lives. Many of the 'stories' (the people behind the stories) from the Forgiveness Project website were setting up new organisations designed to educate and promote peace, respect and compassion, all stemming from their own experiences. I felt so grateful and privileged to be part of this forgiveness family and to be one among so many motivating and inspiring people.

Doors were beginning to open for me as well, in ways that I had never imagined. Not long after my story had been posted on the website, Marina Cantacuzino contacted me and told me she was writing a book about forgiveness that would contain forty stories from the website, and that her publisher had chosen mine to be included. She asked me if that was OK, to which I replied, 'Of course!' After all, my story was now public on the Internet.

Positive reviews of the book poured in from many sources, including the *Guardian* and Amazon, and again, my story got attention. It even made it across the pond as one of four stories cited in the *Washington Post*'s 'Inspired Life' blog about the book and forgiveness.

I went to the very well attended book launch in London with my sister Geraldine in March 2015. There were a few other 'stories' there too, and it was a real treat to meet and connect with them. During her speech, Marina asked us to put up our hands while she thanked us for sharing our healing stories. I was proud to do so and in no way felt any shame at all.

People approached me at the launch and told me about the effects that reading my story had had on them. One woman told me she had been raped at sixteen and that my story had helped her to realise it wasn't her fault. Several more shared their stories and thanked me for my bravery and courage, and for lighting the way for them. I was moved by the kindness I was shown, and yet I found it a bit strange that people recognised me from my photo and knew who I was, when I had no idea who they were!

I started to get more messages on Facebook from women who had come across my story, had undergone similar experiences to mine and who wanted to thank me for showing them what was possible. This outpouring of support and tremendous feedback got me thinking.

I have been a victim of a crime that leaves you silent, and there is so much that stays hidden in that silence. It not only protects the perpetrators, but it also keeps the victims in the shadows, drowning in their inappropriate guilt. Now, my strength is my voice and I intend to use it, not just for me, but also for others who aren't able to speak up yet.

The first time I spoke out publicly was a television interview I did for a production company on rape and anonymity laws. I flew down to Stansted Airport for the day and was met straight away by the presenter and the cameraman, filming me through the arrivals area! We went to a nearby hotel, where I met the rest of the team, and we carried out the interview with two cameras on me. It lasted about three hours.

I felt surprisingly calm, considering I was being filmed, and it was the first time I had spoken out publicly about being raped; it felt like the right thing to do. The segment was scheduled to be aired on the TV programme *Dispatches* on Channel 4 in the UK. The presenter asked me about what had happened to me, and wanted to know my thoughts on whether men who have been accused of rape should have the right to remain anonymous. Afterwards, one of the cameramen asked me if I had done any presenting work. I told him, 'No, I haven't, why do you ask?' He said it was because I was so calm. I told him I was surprised by my calm, too!

A charity called The Extra Guest invited me to speak at their annual Conference of Light, held in December 2015 at the University of Keele, located just outside Newcastle-under-Lyme, England. The theme was 'Making Peace with the Enemy'. Years before, the thought of speaking in front of a few hundred people would have made me mightily nervous, but now I could see the benefits that came from sharing my story and that actually, it was not about me anymore. So I agreed.

When it was my turn to speak, I felt a bit nervous, but once I got past the first sentence, I was really OK and the words just flowed from my mouth. I spoke unscripted for thirty-five minutes. A fire alarm went off in the middle of my talk and we all had to leave the building for about five minutes, but when we got back in, I was able to pick up where I'd left off with no problems. My talk concluded with people in the audience asking me questions and I really enjoyed answering them: it showed me that they were truly engaged and interested.

The best part of the evening was meeting people during the tea break; they approached me and told me how much they identified with my story and that theirs were similar in many ways. And for the first time outside of a professional context, and because of hearing my story, a man shared his experience of sexual abuse with me. One woman told me that she couldn't come up with many words at the time apart from telling me that what I had to say was 'important' – those few words have stayed with me.

From that event, I learned that I'm ready to go out and speak to people, and that I'm not afraid or ashamed to talk about what happened to me in any way; I felt very supported and, again, calm. I have since been asked to take part in more events and speak more, which I'm looking forward to doing, especially after seeing the impact it has on people.

Two days after my return from Keele, I conducted a radio interview with BBC Radio 5 Live, which was broadcasting daily programmes on forgiveness all week. The theme on that particular day was forgiveness and health. I spoke to the presenters and a doctor about how forgiveness has positively affected my health and the difference it has made in my life. It went really well and, once more, I felt calm and relaxed.

A playwright who is working on a play about sexual violence has also contacted me. After reading my story on the Internet, she decided that she would like to try and weave my experience through her work in some way. We are still in discussions about the best way to approach it. And The Forgiveness Project's sister group in America has invited me to speak over there, if they can arrange the funding.

I never intended to write a book, but it wasn't long after I met Marian Partington that words about my story began flying around and around my head, much as they had when Emahó encouraged me to write it all down for him. It came to me that not only should I speak about what had happened to me, but I should also write it out again, in greater detail, and with the intention of reaching a broader audience.

Most of the time, it has felt as if the book has been writing itself, with the words just flowing from my fingertips whenever I sit down to write. At times it's been hard for me to recognise the person I've been writing about, given where I am today; she feels so distant to me now. But I'm no longer that scared person, trying to cover up my emotions in order to appear normal to everyone who knows me; I'm no longer trying to hide my extraordinary experience.

In the past, I would often wonder why this had happened to me – and I don't know if I'll ever know. However, I do believe that everything happens for a purpose; I know my story has helped many people and I intend to carry on. If you had told me even just a few years ago that I would be speaking publicly and writing a book, I would never have believed it. I am now learning to trust that life knows what it is doing.

I would never wish what happened to me on anyone, but I wouldn't change it either now, even if I could. My journey led me to meet Steven, my best friend and soulmate, and between us, we have produced three amazing daughters. For him and our girls, I am grateful beyond words. He loved me when I thought I was unlovable, which in turn taught me to love myself. I know with complete certainty that my journey would not have been the same without him.

It feels like my journey of understanding, processing and

healing has ended, and that this path of speaking out is my new beginning and direction. No more staying quiet and no more shame: I'm proud of who I am.

Being gang-raped altered my life in so many ways, but it also woke me up and put me on a journey of self-discovery. All the work I did landed me back in my body, which I left on that night for many years. It was only by facing my worst nightmares that I could integrate and accept what was done to me, to finally achieve peace with it all.

Ultimately, what helped me most was my choice of forgiveness, for both my rapists and myself. At times, it was harder for me to muster forgiveness than to face most of my fears, but it was an act of self-liberation and of self-empowerment, and it's been a great relief.

Forgiveness has also provided me with almost overwhelming gratitude and thankfulness. I'm so very thankful I wasn't killed that night – too many women aren't that fortunate. I have rebuilt my life, and when I look around me, I see I have so much, both internally and externally. Those feelings of gratitude have amplified my life, given it more colour.

I can't offer anyone a step-by-step programme to help them heal; they will have to find their own way. But I do know this: we can get past anything that happens to us if we choose to, because ultimately, it's not what happens to us that's important, but how we deal with and react to it. We are so much more than what happens to us, we are always stronger than we think.

I understand now that we are not our bodies or even our minds; I know that whatever they did to me, they couldn't take away or crush the real essence of me, which is very much alive and stronger than ever today. That fire inside me never went out; I just had to find it again.

I will continue to use my experience in positive ways, to educate others about what can happen to people living on this planet, and I pray that one day sexual violence will be a thing of the past.

I used to think I could never talk about what happened to me, but now I refuse to be silenced. I hope that by simply speaking out, I can help to reduce the stigma of rape and incite cultural change; it is possible.

I don't live in the past, chained to what happened to me; I live my life looking forward, and I will spread my story with its message of hope, healing and strength to as many people as I can. I want people to know what they are capable of and that we are all so much more than one night.

ACKNOWLEDGEMENTS

I have been supported by so many wonderful people throughout the journey of writing my memoir, and *Unbroken* would not have been possible without their help.

It all started with Emahó encouraging me to find my voice by writing out my story for him, which opened doors for me and led me onto the path of writing a book. I could never have imagined that those few pages would lead to *Unbroken* and I will always be grateful.

Richard Benjamin started to edit my book free of charge, but due to other commitments, he was no longer able to continue. I won't forget his kindness.

My friend Joe Parente, who works as an editor, stepped in where Richard left off and I couldn't have produced the book without him. We worked together so well even though an ocean separated us; he edited alongside me as the book was unfolding chapter by chapter.

As soon as I had finished a chapter I would send it to my friend, Annie Gupta, who constantly encouraged me to keep going when I was losing faith and questioned whether I should continue writing my book.

I am grateful to those who supported me by reading an early draft and writing an endorsement, including Alexander McCall Smith, Arno Arr Michaelis IV, Gary Lewis, Judith Staff, Lorraine McIntosh, Marian Partington, Marina Cantacuzino and Peter Woolf.

Thank you to the team at John Blake Books, especially Emma Stokes, who was working as a publishing intern when she received my submission and believed in me from the very start.

Euan Thorneycroft kindly advised and guided me through the contract process despite not being my agent, and I'm very grateful as I was clueless.

Thank you to my many friends and family for being so supportive. You all know who you are and how much you mean to me. I thank my mum for her courage in allowing me to share her story, and my dad who showed me what hope and resilience looks like by how he lived his life.

My children are three of my greatest achievements in my life. I am so proud of Anna, Mimi and Leila and I thank them for all their constant love, pride and encouragement. I could not have written this book without the support of Steven, my husband, who believed in me from the first moment we met and taught me what unconditional love is.

I felt very strongly that the full details of the rape should be included in my book, and I thank my editors James Hodgkinson and Jane Donovan for allowing this. I know it's not an easy read at times, but how do we ever make changes or gain new understanding if we shy away from all that is difficult and uncomfortable, and only focus on the good in life?

If anyone had told me years ago that one day I would be writing a book, doing radio and TV interviews or speaking publicly I would never have believed it. But it was the courage of others speaking out that helped me to find my voice, which is now my power. It has taken me a long time to find my voice but I won't be silenced now.

Lastly, I thank all the other survivors out there who have made contact and shared their many stories with me. I know my story is one of many but I hope by writing and speaking about it that I can help to break down the silence, shame and stigma of sexual violence with the hope of changing our culture too.

I also want people to know that we are not just the events in our lives; we are so much more. And, if we choose to, we really can learn to overcome anything that happens to us in life.

ACKNOWLEDGEMENTS

The Forgiveness Project is a UK-based charity working with stories as tools for change. Collecting and sharing real stories of transformation, it seeks to foster tolerance, build empathy and give people the opportunity to break the cycle of harm. www.theforgivenessproject.com / info@theforgivenessproject.com

Rape Crisis Freephone helpline: 0808 802 9999

Find Madeleine Black on Twitter: @madblack65

madeleineblack.co.uk

©Nicky Johnston

ABOUT THE AUTHOR

Sharing her story opened doors for Madeleine in ways she never imagined and the invitations started to pour in. She has taken part in both TV and radio interviews and has been invited to speak at conferences, events and schools.

She recognises that she was a victim of a crime that left her silent for many years, but has now found her voice and intends to use it. Not just for her, but for so many who have not yet found theirs.

She is married and lives in Glasgow with her husband, three daughters, her cat, Suki, and dog, Alfie.